DEAD RECKONING

T0344582

DEAD RECKONING

Transatlantic Passages on Europe and America

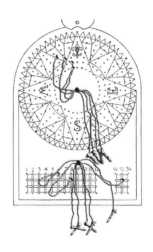

Andrei Guruianu *and* Anthony Di Renzo

excelsior editions

AN IMPRINT OF STATE UNIVERSITY OF NEW YORK PRESS

Published by
STATE UNIVERSITY OF NEW YORK PRESS, ALBANY

© 2016 State University of New York

All rights reserved

Printed in the United States of America

No part of this book may be used or reproduced in any manner whatsoever without written permission. No part of this book may be stored in a retrieval system or transmitted in any form or by any means including electronic, electrostatic, magnetic tape, mechanical, photocopying, recording, or otherwise without the prior permission in writing of the publisher.

EXCELSIOR EDITIONS IS AN IMPRINT OF
STATE UNIVERSITY OF NEW YORK PRESS

For information, contact
State University of New York Press, Albany, NY
www.sunypress.edu

Production, Laurie D. Searl
Marketing, Anne M. Valentine

Library of Congress Cataloging-in-Publication Data

Guruianu, Andrei.
  Dead reckoning : transatlantic passages on Europe and America / Andrei Guruianu and Anthony Di Renzo.
    pages cm
  ISBN 978-1-4384-6112-0 (pbk. : alk. paper) —
  ISBN 978-1-4384-6114-4 (e-book)
  I. Di Renzo, Anthony, 1960– II. Title.
  PS3607.U567D43 2016
  814'.6—dc23

                                                              2015027724

10 9 8 7 6 5 4 3 2 1

for

MILAN KUNDERA,

who made beauty and laughter out of exile

APHORISM 124

In the Horizon of the Infinite

We have left the land and have embarked. We have burned our bridges behind us—indeed, we have gone farther and destroyed the land behind us. Now, little ship, look out! Beside you is the ocean: to be sure, it does not always roar, and at times it lies spread out like silk and gold and reveries of graciousness. But hours will come when you will realize that it is infinite and that there is nothing more awesome than infinity. Oh, the poor bird that felt free and now strikes the walls of this cage! Woe, when you feel homesick for the land as if it had offered more freedom—and there is no longer any "land."

—Friedrich Nietzsche, *The Gay Science*

Contents

Antonio

To the Reader

THIS EXCHANGE—"writes" of passage, if you will—began during the summer of 2013. Consider it a log from two immigrant writers, a poet and an essayist, marooned in the doldrums between the Old and New Worlds. For years, we sailed under the flag of phantom allegiances, pretending that our home ports (Romania and Italy) still existed. Without the illusion of safe harbor, mariners go mad at sea. Even Odysseus, the wiliest of wanderers, needed the fiction of Ithaca.

Hope filled our sails. We traveled ever westward to the New Atlantis of America. One day, however, like the crew in *The Rime of the Ancient Mariner*:

> We stuck, nor breath or motion;
>
> As idle as a painted ship
>
> Upon a painted ocean.

Forced to abandon ship, we found shelter and supplies on a nearby deserted island. Ever since, we have been studying out-of-date maps to chart a new course to God knows where. No luck, so far, but perhaps our notes will become a survival manual for fellow castaways like you.

Please pardon our accents. English is not our first language, but it is the language that we are compelled to write in. It baffles us, but as

Sicilian American scholar and writer Edvige Giunta observes, "Living in another culture and writing in another language sometimes offer an intellectual and creative freedom that living in your own culture and writing in your own language do not." Perhaps we need to maintain our foreignness to access and jot these thoughts.

Dead Reckoning, the title of our book, is a nautical term. When instruments fail or when astronomical observation is impossible, navigators calculate a ship's position using the distance and direction traveled. This computation is based on compass readings, known speed, and figures culled from charts, logs, and almanacs. What seems an exact science is actually desperate guesswork. Navigators must make allowances for drift from the wind and currents, but these factors remain unpredictable and ultimately unknowable. In this sense, dead reckoning can function as an analogy for postmodernism, Europe's and America's collective groping in the dark because the West has lost or destroyed its bearings.

For those still recovering from the atrocities of the twentieth century, however, whether under Fascism or Communism, dead reckoning has an even grimmer meaning: toting up the butcher's bill of war and genocide. This is another, less frequently discussed side of postmodernism. The dead always have exacted guilt from the living, just as the living always have denied their complicity in past evil. Our generation, however, is the first to deny the meaning or even the possibility of history. This is foolish and arrogant. Despite the distractions of technology and commerce, nothing will spare us from a day of reckoning. The Furies always settle their accounts, whether or not they use Microsoft spreadsheets.

These concerns inspired the following poems and essays. It has been a harrowing odyssey—less a circumnavigation of the globe than a salvage expedition in a naval graveyard. Significantly, our collaboration fell between the centennials of two maritime disasters: the wreck of the *Titanic* (April 14, 1912) and the sinking of the *Lusitania* (May 7, 1915). Both foreshadowed the greater shipwreck of Western civilization, from which Europe and America, we believe, are still floundering in shark-infested waters.

Thank you for allowing two amateur navigators the leeway to chart these tangents. We recognize, however, that in the wide Sargasso Sea of Internet culture, any book must be a message in a bottle. But this is the writer's perennial dilemma. "We work in the dark," said Henry James. "We do what we can. We give what we have. Our doubt is our passion, and our passion is our task. The rest is the madness of art."

Andrei Guruianu
Anthony Di Renzo

I

Memory, You Savage Triumph

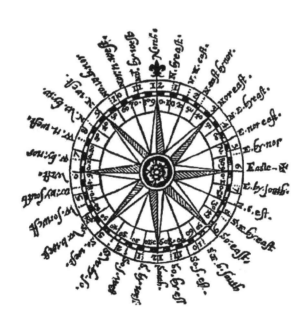

Andrei

A Blueprint for Memory

MEMORY, MOTHER OF THE MUSES, also suckles the Furies. For poets and exiles, memory is both a divine inspiration and a punishing obsession.

Imagine a simple sketch of a house whose foundation has been laid out. Now the artist begins to raise the building from the ground, putting up the supporting walls. The horizontal line suggests a ceiling. As he toils away at the upper section, the house's foundation begins to blur, slowly being erased until it disappears, and the artist must go back and fill it in again, obsessively retracing his steps. As he moves back and forth between beginning and forward progress ad infinitum, we must ask ourselves, will he ever finish?

This paradox is impossible in a world of brick and mortar, but not necessarily in memory, where the present is not experienced as a discrete series of linear events. Instead, it exists as a mirror image of the past, each moment forming a parallel history of itself, just as subway passengers will catch their reflections in the windows of a passing train going in the opposite direction. A life, doubly exposed.

The realization that such moments appear and disappear in that same impossible-to-picture instant we call the *now* could be maddening. And so we are left with our only option, to rescue it from the catacombs of abstraction, if such a reality should have any meaning. In other words, we need something to ground ourselves, a space in which we might find our bearings. We must give shape to memory while acknowledging its power to shape us.

Alain de Botton, the Jewish Swiss philosopher, demonstrates how physical place defines our very existence, in *The Architecture of Happiness*:

> The house has grown into a knowledgeable witness. It has been party to early seductions, it has watched homework being written,

it has observed swaddled babies freshly arrived from the hospital, it has been surprised in the middle of the night by whispered conferences in the kitchen. It has experienced winter evenings when its windows were as cold as bags of frozen peas and midsummer dusks when its brick walls held the warmth of freshly baked bread.

It has provided not only physical but psychological sanctuary. It has been a guardian of identity. Over the years, its owners have returned from periods away and, on looking around them, remembered who they were.

Place, I would add, not only helps us remember who we *were*, but also who we *are*. The acts of shaping and being shaped by place also happen simultaneously. Likewise, memory always comes to us in the shape of place, having both tangible and imagined coordinates. We put faces, events, and emotions in coordinates of space that provide a certain logical grammar to remembrance. There can be no other way. As Martin Heidegger observed, "poetically man dwells." Metaphor houses consciousness. Whether real or fabricated, memory takes place *inside* space and therefore takes the shape of that space so that it might be called up by the imagination.

Or as Gaston Bachelard puts it in *The Poetics of Space*:

All really inhabited space bears the essence of the notion of home.... [T]he imagination functions in this direction whenever the human being has found the slightest shelter: we shall see the imagination build walls of impalpable shadows, comfort itself with the illusion of protection—or, just the contrary, tremble behind thick walls, mistrust the staunchest ramparts. In short, in the most interminable of dialectics, the sheltered being gives perceptible limits to his shelter.

Bachelard's connection between *home* and *imagination* suggests how and why exiles use words and images to construct an interior country. After all, de Botton's house (if it still exists) provides only a physical sanctuary. The uprooted man, expelled from his literal home, must find shelter in the imaginary cloister of memory—where contradictions and conflicts are met, reckoned with, and reconciled. Whether stumbling through actual tunnels or bumping our heads against imaginary ceilings, he is then contained and guided at all times by imagination, the slippery notion of memory and its limitations.

Naturally, we often resist its limiting tendencies and attempt to work our way out of its claws—that obsessive "grip of memory" that would drag us down or backward through the cobwebbed alleys of the past. Such a rebellion nonetheless, and necessarily, takes on similar characteristics as the original structure—we need foundation, stability, we need a space within which we can act. And since the future does not yet exist, we must not only rely on the walls that hold up our storefront of memory, but also actively participate in their construction (as the perpetually frustrated house artist). Otherwise we risk their deterioration and subsequent collapse at our feet—and we'll have nothing to stand on, not even an illusion.

Return through a Gap in Time

To the school of ruins and acquired gravitas. Past fish with blackened eyelids swimming through the crumble of districts. Memory, you savage triumph, I followed you through secret tunnels, under false ceilings, wearing only sorrow's wrinkled shirt, one lonely black sock. Like a fool I thought I could pass for native here. We kept bumping into each other in the rat's nest of alleys, in seedy bars where the music was slow and old fashioned and the players too much into the wine. The glow of each face clung to me like a superstition. Names became constellations on the black sky of my mouth. I fled toward water, the perfectly aligned blue margins where penciled in stars were suffocating on the urban summertime. Forgive me what I cannot, I said to them in their dying hour, I am preoccupied with the worst of my successes. I am connecting dots. I am building a dam. And after that, if they haven't carted off every last block, maybe one of the four walls.

Propaganda of the Self

And we will, as a lesson in what constitutes aesthetics, feed on paintings of bread, secured to the village walls with a knot of spit and casual indifference. We will pass the night with the old tea drinkers on the terrace overlooking crowds below fast-forwarding through moments of eternal beauty. Mere animals of convalescent passion throwing pennies at the clairvoyant blind man selling numbers for the lotto on an everyday street corner. Where the little girl by his side does not fold easily beneath the weight of night—that is until the belly bites the feverish tongue and trees begin to show their black horns gilded in a string of light.

♲

At the crux of first and last vision of solitude, one of us will break with the solemn circus, another will be claimed by some voluptuous breach of time. All of them commonplace funerals that make for a good excuse to keep your head down and your hand in your overcoat pocket. The little girl's hand orphaned from itself reaching for your own, for what it might hold inside, for what it doesn't know that it wants.

And all that she asks, aiming her caged voice like a dagger, is whether you are happy and if your heart has ever been broken—for that she assigns a number that dangles at the gate of your own mortality like an umbilical noose... The wind snatches it and buries it in the night and before you can argue she pulls out another number, another chance, sober with the weight of business and self-pity. The wind snatches it and buries it in the night.

♲

If only I could turn back to retrieve it, to pry it from her unkissed mouth! But there is always someone standing between me. Even more between me and that Eastern harbor of creation—the crowd surging along as if mad, rubbing against the walls, stumbling every now and then over the occasional shiny premonition, dangling like a cheap pearl from a roadside stand.

From All Points East

If you get a postcard from here it will bear a rose at the height of its bloom, possibly a snapshot of the village chapel on a sunny afternoon. Note that its high windows signify compartments of the soul, the heart turned inside out, poured out, the single mind in a moment of space.

In a slanted scrawl someone will have written *wish you were here*, which, of course, is nothing more than a figure of speech meaning come on over, take a long hard look around you, see the high water marks on every home, the boards rotten but somehow holding by a thread. Meaning please do not forget us as soon as you turn your back—

we, of all people, know what it's like because we've cried wolf so many times before that we can't even tell at times where the old story ends and where the new one begins; you know the one, it's been in all the papers, flower girls on street corners, so fragile they appear capable of being wounded by the moon. How they sell their perfect cellophane bouquets, masks for any occasion, the wink and smile that says *Thank you* or *I'm sorry*, for whatever you will—

while off to the side old women nod away on wooden boxes, legs sprawled over trampled petals of yesterday's unwanted blossoms. See them sitting there, sleep-praying what remains of their days into salvation. Notice the elbow patches on worn sweaters, the stockings fraying at the knees—

how typical, how kitsch this photograph would look next to the other ones you keep inside an old cigar box for posterity, so that when you pull it out after too many years have passed it will be 1985 all over again, the same old communists still feeding on sausage and cheese.

And what's that in the corner, you ask, barely a blur of skin and bones? Just a lame dog, chained to the walnut tree, young boys walking by picking up sticks, learning to ration out fear.

Antonio

Laughing in the Ruins (Pt. 1)

"THE STRUGGLE OF MAN AGAINST POWER," said the Czech writer Milan Kundera, "is the struggle of memory against forgetting." But the drive for power springs from man's inability to accept impermanence. This is part of "the propaganda of the self." We construct tombstones, cairns, pyramids to defy time, knowing full well that they are doomed to crumble. All monuments collapse under the weight of futility. All regimes deny this fact. The results are inevitably laughable.

Nowhere is this truer than Rome, my second home. Cat ladies feed strays amid the Forum's broken columns. A hag operates a beauty parlor inside the Arch of Gallienus. Prostitutes fellate clients beneath Nero's Aqueduct. Sponsors project ads on the Coliseum. Antiquity is powerless against the cunning of appetite. Foragers pick capers on the Aurelian Wall between Porta San Lorenzo and the Ministry of Aeronautics. Beside the Colossus of Constantine, vendors sell *supplì*: fried rice balls stuffed with mincemeat, tomato sauce, and mozzarella. Customers raise a single finger and imitate the emperor's shattered hand.

Left alone, fragments can be beautiful. Giovanni Piranesi, the eighteenth-century artist, celebrated Rome's ruins in a series of breathtaking etchings. He wed decay and design, chaos and order, transience and endurance. Nineteenth- and twentieth-century nationalists wanted more. Revolutionaries such as Giuseppe Mazzini and poets such as Giosuè Carducci were convinced that they could rescue the shards of the past from the bulldozer of foreign oppression and the piledriver of the Industrial Revolution. Like Amphion, they would sing the stones into place and form an Eternal City of the imagination. Benito Mussolini exploited this cult of antiquity. Palazzo Braschi, home of the Museo di Roma, would become the Fascist Party's headquarters.

All dictatorships rely on ambitious restoration and preservation projects. While planning the 1936 Summer Olympics, Albert Speer designed a building that would leave behind aesthetically pleasing ruins, if it eventually collapsed. These ruins, he claimed, would last far longer than the original structure, without any subsequent maintenance. Speer called his concept *Ruinenwert* (Ruin Value), but the idea actually dates back to Goethe's *Italian Journey*. German Romanticism valued classical ruins. Nazism ruined classical values. Posing as a Master Builder, Hitler reduced Europe to rubble. After *götterdämmerung*, a Berlin cabaret comic joked: "Even the ruins have been ruined."

The catastrophe of World War II birthed the postmodern world, a postapocalyptic culture in which all memory fragments and all words fail. Nothing remains but the shimmering play of colored lights on a vista of shattered glass. Collectively suffering from post-traumatic stress condition, we seem incapable of rebuilding our world, caught between frenetic denial and paralyzing despair. How can we value the ruins of our civilization when we continue to ruin its values?

Americans respond to this crisis by turning the past into a theme park and by investing their energy in the posthuman future. They imagine building a chain of Holiday Inns on Mars or downloading their brains onto a computer. Determined to preserve a mythical innocence at all cost, they turn their back on an appalling record of slavery, genocide, war, and economic and ecological carnage. By necessity, therefore, they denigrate and bulldoze their ruins, calling this destruction "urban renewal."

Europeans, both victims and perpetrators of centuries of bloodshed, know this strategy is self-defeating. They know that they will never recover from history unless they acknowledge and atone for past atrocities. But they also have learned, at an appalling cost, that fixating on guilt and horror turns life into a tale told by an idiot, full of sound and fury, signifying nothing. Fortunately, their genius for ironic endurance best expresses itself through surreal humor.

Andrei

Echoes of a Remembered Sentiment

> *Instant coffee for the old times.*
> *The aftertaste of a full moon in the mouth.*

I stand again between two mirrors because I like to see every side of myself. When I walk out the door I take my aloneness with me like a kerchief at the breast. A freshly pressed flower. On the fugitive highway angels pluck their feathers passing as familiar others. Only they do not speak like me. And because they cannot fly they stagger. Fall forward. Something about that feels like the memory I commit every night in my dreams. I bend down, lift up an angel by his skeleton arm and I say *Come back with me, rest in my home for a while, I have some lunchmeat and homemade jam, we can buy some dark bread on the way, a spoonful of coffee for the old times.* Without changing course he says in the language of a needle's eye, *Thanks friend, but everything is impossible yesterday. Go back and cover your mirrors. There's nothing left for you there. I meant to tell you but it happened so long ago and I've had much on my mind.* And with that he tears off the last of his feathers, slips on a hat, and disappears into the crowd.

Truth and Tangents (or What Becomes Art)

All day there were celebrations, street protests and celebrations. They seemed to belong together—graduation songs and banners, tears of a last embrace that stretched from *Cişmigiu* to *Piaţa Universitaţii*. I saw mothers before they were mothers and they looked just like the pictures. I walked among the street cleaners and dropouts, runaways and dissidents, every color of a crooked deal.

On each corner (blind intersection of time), the same old tale: mythos of an archaic city, this all-too-real city, farce of a carnival at twilight. Same characters, generational difference: fallen angels littering the walk, the drunks and hobos, literati, last year's fashion resurrected from the dead, the ordinary marginal as it has always been.

And my mother was there too, wearing heels and lipstick, in a corner of the frame, but the focus is soft, the details are vague, though she looks skinny and happy, as someone who imagines the future, ordinary and marginal, as it has always been.

Lipscani

In the heart of Bucharest, the ghost of happy endings. June biting into cobblestones on restoration row. On either side, moonlit stores with musty, yellow postcards, weather-bitten coins, and memories of the war.

A clock without any feet and an obnoxious grin says I'm looking for dry blood in all the wrong places. I walk until the night reminds me of the cold, the dust how thirsty I have been for all these years.

Inside a dirty, miserable pub, the crooked bartender slides a glass my way and leans in confidence, *There is indeed a resurrection in the streets, and you too, old friend, can buy redemption at the court of thieves and well-mannered impostors.*

What could I do but nod and toast the mirror on the wall? Watch the likeness of myself stare back as if he'd never seen me there before.

Antonio

Laughing in the Ruins (Pt. 2)

THE RUIN PUB (*romkocsma* in Hungarian) testifies to the power of human laughter. Found all over Budapest, these bars spring up and sometimes disappear overnight in the courtyards of the old Jewish ghetto, emptied and abandoned during the Holocaust, or in the city's derelict neighborhoods, bombed out and never rebuilt after the Revolution of 1956 or allowed to go to ruin under Goulash Communism, when Hungary was called "the happiest barrack in the Soviet camp."

Street-smart entrepreneurs have perfected a winning formula: Find an abandoned building, add a bar, a dance floor and outdoor seating, throw in a mix of art and Kádárism nostalgia, and encourage patrons to savor desolation. Rather than cover up the surrounding decay, ruin pubs spotlight, even celebrate it, as evident in a popular toast: *"This property is condemned, but so is the human race."*

Budapest's trendiest *romkocsma* is Szimpla Kert, commonly known as Szimpla. Lonely Planet, the globe's largest travel guide publisher, named it "the third best bar in the world." The pub's appearance belies its status. Located at 14 Kazinczy Utca, this crumbling two-story building seems fit only for the wrecking ball. Most of its windows are boarded up and a thick layer of dirt and grime has settled into its leprous façade. Potted plants line a corroded wrought-iron balcony overlooking the street while a jaunty but jaundiced yellow sign hangs in the doorway below.

Push past the splintered front door, however, and grope down the dimly lit hallway and you will come to a large, open-air courtyard. Colored string lights, broken furniture, and a bicycle or two hang suspended above, while scenes from a black and white art-house film flicker on the cracked back wall. Off to the side sits a rusted old Trabant, a compact car made in East Germany during the Cold War. The courtyard opens onto a maze of rooms, each decorated differently. In one, fossilized computer monitors and television sets are mounted to the walls. In another, a split bathtub serves as a makeshift seating area.

More than a bar, Szimpla is also a café, a salon, a bistro, a town hall, and a theme park. The kitchen serves *lángos*, Hungarian pizza topped with onion, bacon, sausage, and sour cream, and hosts a traditional farmers' market on Sundays. Success, however, may have doomed it. Like other *romkocsmas*, Szimpla has become an unwitting catalyst of gentrification, pulling yuppies into formerly run-down areas of the city and attracting the attention of real estate developers. Old buildings are being torn down and replaced with upscale apartment complexes and glitzy restaurants and boutiques. This trend threatens to remake Budapest into a city where ruin pubs can no longer credibly exist. When that happens, many residents believe, Budapest will lose its soul.

A civic organization called "ÓVÁS!" ("Protest!") opposes this string of demolitions. Ruin pub owners gladly side with academics and preservationists to maintain the city's bohemian scene, but they will be the first to admit that they never set out to rescue Budapest's old neighborhoods. "We didn't save the historical building on purpose," admits Titusz Badonics, a technician who works at Instant, a ruin pub that opened in 2008 in the city's sixth district. "We just use it to do something which looks great in these kind of buildings. We make something until it's gone."

But isn't that true of all of us? We all make something until it's gone, never fully understanding our motives and never able to see the final results. Creation often results from accident, not choice. If we achieve anything worthwhile, it is usually unintentional. "Beauty by mistake," Milan Kundera muses in *The Unbearable Lightness of Being*: "the final chapter in the history of beauty."

II

The Art of Exile

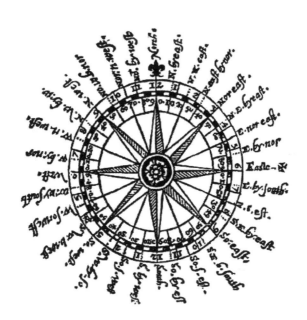

Andrei

Yes, I Am. Maybe.

> For a writer's language, far from being a mere means of expression, is above all a mode of subjective existence and a way of experiencing the world. She needs the language not just to describe things, but to *see* them... A writer's language is not just something she uses, but a constitutive part of what she is. This is why to abandon your native tongue and to adopt another is to dismantle yourself, piece by piece, and then to put yourself together again, in a different form.
>
> —Costica Bradatan,
> "Born Again in a Second Language," *New York Times*

AS AN IMMIGRANT WRITER IN AMERICA, who has largely abandoned his native language, I sometimes feel as if I'm playing my own character, the embodiment of an "I" whom everyone watches from a distance but who is nothing more than a flimsy façade. "Someone is living my life," wrote the Sicilian playwright Luigi Pirandello in his diary, not long before his death. "And I don't know a thing about him."

Sometimes, though, when performing a walk-through of my own play, I truly believe in my own act, as if it weren't an illusion. But it doesn't take much to blur the lines. When strangers ask me to say something in Romanian, or to explain why I no longer write in the "old language," I feel as if I'm asked to perform yet again, to prove myself or to play the expected role. I don't blame them. People want to know: How much of an immigrant are you? If you really are Romanian, present your calling card—the words, the language, the accent.

Because I've been in America long enough, I am no longer aware of the language I use when I write or speak, at least not to the extent that I used to be when I first transitioned from Romanian to English. Unfailingly, though, someone always manages to remind me. Even the most casual query can make me self-conscious. I am reminded of an NPR interview with Nancy Cartwright, the actress best known as the voice of Bart Simpson, in which she discussed the baggage that comes with being an iconic character. She said that the most common request she gets from people is to "Do Bart!" Most of the time, Cartwright humors them with the phrase "Eat my shorts!" or "Don't have a cow, man!" But as soon as these words escape her mouth, she explained, Bart's voice becomes her "real" voice while her natural voice becomes "fake."

For the immigrant or exile, this bizarre ventriloquism is not a career but a necessity. We are asked to perform (freely or otherwise) to better adapt to circumstance. The number of years away from our homeland hardly matters. Acting has become second nature, an ingrained mechanism, to the extent that the lines can become so blurred that one can no longer distinguish between past and present. Instead, the two form a twisted but continuous loop called reality. This Möbius strip is the permanent immigrant condition.

The paradox of the Möbius strip, a two-dimensional sheet with only one surface, points to the difference between Eastern and Western thought. Western thought, rigid and set in its ways, enforces delineations. Certain laws shall not be broken. That's just the way things are. Eastern thought, which allows for flexibility and continuity, is less structured but still disciplined. Exile is endurance training in finding a middle ground that can be inhabited between the two. Ultimately, we learn to accept that the old ways of thinking might not necessarily work anymore. Rigidity defines monuments but life demands flexibility.

Subsequently, as the alien begins taking on roots in a new language, he also learns to bend and negotiate, to compromise and improvise. Transience and contingency require a Zen practice, but this rarely leads to bliss and enlightenment. Few things are more painfully unnatural than "naturalization." By necessity, then, all immigrants live in a kind of permanent exile, whether self-imposed or otherwise. No gain comes without a loss. That much is obvious, and that much is made certain by the necessity of living between worlds where the border between past and present, old and new selves, is always being redefined. Under such conditions, life becomes a constant haggle with customs inspectors.

All they require, thankfully, is the secret password. When on cue I say, "*Ce faci?*" (How are you?) or, "*Bine ai venit*" (Welcome) to someone who wants to hear what Romanian sounds like, a secret gate seems to swing open and I finally appear as a concrete being, albeit one with a predefined and preloaded label—which, because it is reduced to a known quantity, is rendered familiar and therefore harmless. In other words, I become a copy of a copy that someone remembers seeing once on a PBS special, that paragon of cultural dissemination. Luckily, if you missed it, there are repeats, or TiVo. And every time the special plays, we multiply but remain exactly the same, charged with the preservation of an image of history, culture on late-night parade—the projection of an identity marked and fixed by signifiers.

In the end, that is the biggest lie the exile is forced to tell, and it always begins with "I am. . ." As easy and as painful as pulling an old line out of a tired repertoire performed to indulgent applause. In those moments, whether Cartwright performs Bart or Guruianu performs Andrei, both she and I become someone else. She is no longer Nancy, mother of two. She is not even a Prime time Emmy–winning voice actress playing an iconic pop character. She *is* Bart Simpson, an animated ten-year-old boy, more real to most adult viewers than their own middle-school children.

Likewise, through my own voiceover, I become—to a large extent and to the exclusion of everything else—a cartoon immigrant, a two-dimensional foreigner. Amit Majmudar, in his *New York Times* opinion piece "Am I an 'Immigrant Writer,'" puts it this way:

> Notice how many celebrated minority writers of our time—Mr. Díaz, Chimamanda Ngozi Adichie, Jhumpa Lahiri—tend to write inside their own communities. One explanation may well be the nature of realism, which is (for now) literary fiction's dominant

mode: the artistic need for observed detail, and the tendency of literary novelists to tweak their personal experiences into fiction.

Write what you know, young writers are taught. This may well reinforce, and be reinforced by, our sense of a writer's being an authority only on his or her own community, his or her own people.

So, in a paradoxical way, the freedom to write about your own experience turns into a restriction on the subject matter permissible to you. Your selling point governs how you are perceived.

Should I choose not to play by those rules, what might I lose? Should I choose to play the game, what have I already lost? Either way, we all seem to need better representation. That's the only way to survive show biz.

Some Call It a Performance

Small yard, two gypsy girls half naked chasing a white chicken. They are flailing at the air with a rod. Their black eyes shine like a mad dog's rolling back into their skulls.

☾

A young boy dirty from his head down to his bare feet is pulling through the dust a toy car without any wheels. He smiles as I pass to show that he is harmless. There are lines carved on his face, black rivers that end at his chin. He wears a pink shirt that at one time used to be a beautiful, deep cherry red. A mother's kiss diluted through the years. He puts out a brown hand to pluck the storm about to break any moment. I hurry by and pocket my fists to show there is no time to waste. I wonder if he believes me, if he believes in the passing of time the same way silence passes between us. If he sees the fear in my own two eyes. So I act natural, I make a show of being happy and carefree. I look down into the dirt and kick a small rock all the way home.

Of Marionettes

For safekeeping we took pictures of our shadows. The clouds kept ticking by above, making it difficult to focus. One of us came out without an arm, another was missing a leg. The stains on the sidewalk made for uneven eyes, black and all-knowing. How I wish I could question them, hold a knife to their skin and make them talk. What did you see when you looked through me? What am I, really, when I am me? I moved two feet to the left and took another picture—no lopsided eye, no tongue, no crooked teeth—it could have been any one of us, and no one was sad because of it.

The Faces We Wear

Imagine that from a distance we must all look somewhat like children, at once petulant and giddy with wine, mere interruptions in the syntax of history, brief incisions to the infinite. And how we must look holding on so dearly to our place in line! How we grip the strings that lead us there! If you listen hard enough, you could hear the ground shake as a million hands bang away at the national song, voices tearing through a dialect learned a long time ago. Before speech. Before language. In some forgotten village watched over by a frontline of trees and ungoverned fields. In some village that was once good enough when there wasn't anything else, not even the word for it.

☙

For how long can one remain loyal to the fate he's given? *Oh, if only I could split myself to encompass more than a single life.* I've thought it and you've thought it, and for this we sacrifice the present. This is what we kneel for in our dreams like impostors—though I'm certain that blood spills for no one but the ground it falls on. Not a stray, salutary drop to lessen the straits of an ordinary destiny—mornings or nights getting dressed in silence, under suit of darkness, after making love. As the wise will tell you, *Because we make our beds before we're ready to lie down, the only thing left to do is lie down.* After all, the great months that lie ahead are already measured and counted; and the one who knows exactly how many are left walks on among us forced to wear a disguise.

Antonio

A Hole in the Sky (Pt. 1)

ON THE STREETS OF PALERMO AND CATANIA, as well as dozens of provincial towns, puppeteers perform grotesque adaptions of the *Oresteia* or Carolingian epics. Ragged children squeal and clap, while American tourists, better dressed but no less naive, smile and consult their guidebooks. But adult Sicilians, wearing the black of perpetual mourning, sigh and shake their heads. What a comedown for gods and heroes! Once adored and obeyed, now jerked around to entertain strangers and vagrants! But we all must make a living in this world. Someone behind the scenes always pulls our strings.

As a boy, I attended similar marionette shows at Papa Manteo's on Mulberry Street. My Sicilian mother wished to expose me to this dying tradition. After the Risorgimento, she explained, legislators and educators had frowned upon such plays because they were presented in the Sicilian language and extolled Sicilian history. Both were officially discouraged in favor of the Italian language, national unity, and later Fascism. Some puppeteers emigrated to the New World to make a living in urban Sicilian colonies. Agrippino Manteo, born near Catania, had brought his troupe from Mendoza, Argentina, to New York's Little Italy after World War I. His grandson Mike allowed me to handle the family's life-size puppets.

When I moved from ethnic Brooklyn to the whitebread suburbs of Freehold, New Jersey, I decided to stage my own marionette show. Mamma and I built a tiny theater on our patio. Against my father's advice, I printed flyers in crayon and invited the entire neighborhood. The paladins in tinfoil and gold tinsel baffled my playmates and the Sicilian barked behind the scenes must have sounded like gibberish to their parents. The audience remained polite. My kindergarten teacher burbled compliments. Then disaster struck. As the Normans routed the

Scaracens at the Battle of Misilmeri, the backdrop tore and completely exposed me. Children pointed and jeered, adults laughed, but I was too shocked to react. It was as if the sky had split. My face burned, and tears stung my eyes.

After this public humiliation, I gradually stopped speaking Sicilian, much to Mamma's distress. I did not fully comprehend what had happened to me, however, until I read Luigi Pirandello's novel *The Late Mattia Pascal*. The great Sicilian writer compares life to a puppet show and existential anxiety to a torn paper sky.

Suppose, he says, if at the climax of a puppet show, just when the marionette playing Orestes is about to avenge his father's death and kill his mother and her lover, a hole appeared in the paper sky of the scenery. What would happen? Orestes would become distracted and then obsessed by that hole. He would still feel his desire for revenge and still want passionately to achieve it, but his eyes always would return to that hole, from which more demons would escape than from Pandora's Box and crowd the stage. They would mock Orestes until he became helpless; and at that moment, Orestes would become Hamlet (or worse, a parody of Hamlet). "There's the whole difference between ancient and modern tragedy," Pirandello concludes, "a hole torn in a paper sky."

Lucky marionettes, over whose wooden heads the false sky has no holes! For this misbegotten generation of Pinocchios, disowned by Geppetto and abandoned by the Blue Fairy, the backdrop has been utterly shredded. Postmodern academics, gainfully employed and protected from the consequences of do-it-yourself nihilism, consider this devastating condition a prelude to universal liberation. Ordinary people know better. Without scripts, props, or direction, human culture does not inspire improvisation but terminal stage fright or compulsive hamming. We freeze or mug but cannot act.

"Without the aid of prejudice and custom," William Hazlitt said, "I should not be able to find my way across the room; nor know how to conduct myself in any circumstances, nor what to feel in any relation of life." Hazlitt wrote these words in 1830, when the Industrial Revolution, the engine born from the scientific and political revolutions of the previous century, had begun demolishing traditional Western values at full steam. A political radical, Hazlitt was no friend of the Old Order; but he understood and respected the human need for beauty and meaning, which is why he championed Romanticism. Music, painting, and poetry, however, could not patch the rift in the sky. Over the past 180 years, it has gotten only bigger. Why don't we repair it?

Andrei

Because We Are Meant to Be Forgotten

In the dark literature of your own curiosity there is space set aside
where you can dissect the immutable—the sick, misguided tedium that
covers all like an umbrella. With enough practice you can step to the
very edge and watch yourself swim in the fog of blessed light, which is
no light at all, but a vessel straddling the singular statistics—as beautiful as they are sad—a fragrant leaf, the chatoyant, coffee in the flavored
morning for the ones about to change without knowing it—for they
are the ones bored with love and with desire, haunted by the naked eye
seeing and not seeing what is given us—simplicity of wind and moon-
light through the branches, pure thoughts that are more like things,
like a stone that doesn't want its meaning to be known—for a stone is
meant to be seen and forgotten so that it might be seen again; a stone
has no philosophy of possession, it cannot perish as we do between the
lines, inside the fever of a single utterance, which, once spoken, lowers
its head in shame—as if condemned for imitation.

Zero-Sum

My father the philosopher builds a temple out of rebar. He stands at the iron gate and takes it in: hollow edifice of angles, intersections, corners you can tear a sleeve on, maybe bleed a while. He counts the change in his pockets but it's not enough. He crams in the wind and clouds, he stuffs the hole in the wall with a pair of jeans and an old button down shirt but it is not enough.

When I was half of what I am and less than that, he used to build me castles out of wood down on the fake green grass of our kitchen. I toppled them with a child's fist that had never known any scars. Now I build my temples out of rusted keys and a loose padlock. The keys turn and turn without any resistance but the lock never chokes open. On the other side I watch the ancient continent on fire, the wick burning at both ends. Luckily the days are late in coming here so we live for now on old news and some homemade cabbage rolls. I keep working the keys with one cheek always to the lookout.

My father is an interesting man without any hobbies. He is no longer passionate about anything. The secret is a part-time existence. The lesson is part-time everything. How to preserve states of too-honest emotion. He would make the perfect argument for an American fantasy—ornery, grumbling, my father thinks he can weave new endings to unfortunate beginnings. He played with fire once so he says nothing when the streets are bleeding news into the camera lens. Now he plays the lottery in case God happens to play favorites.

At night, between worn out gums, he sends the world clandestine prayers but he would never admit it. I also hope in silence. I don't want to be the fool who thinks that he could rise among the Babel of voices. Everyone has needs at one time greater than another. It is not science or philosophy or any of the great and lesser religions. Who raised that false tower? And it is also not an endless row of chambers with the keys wrapped tight around our necks. Or at least it shouldn't be.

There are days when I eat and I sleep and somewhere hundreds of miles away I know my father is doing the same. I want to tell him that I understand at least some of it. I realize that we've forgotten how to be more like the animals we are. I know that when I walk my dog she pulls at the leash only by instinct. I pull back and I fight because I don't remember how not to. How to let go. She walks on besides me despite knowing who I am—she does not build her own burdens. She does not have to dismantle anything.

Not-Light

Today I stood shoulder to shoulder with sunlight and we both rose to meet the lips of a winter sky. Cold and brittle. The bones of dusk just beginning to show in the distance and I wanted to kiss those even more. Bone memory softened by time. From the loam came the scent of departed days, warmth of breath, embrace and another embrace; how lovely it seemed once we'd forgotten the past never passes. Lives on and through.

Shoulder to shoulder the sunlight played adagio for no one in particular. Note how the ivory and string comes close to meaning something (imagine birds). Soon it will mean snow and darkness, the not-light. Sometimes it takes a life to know that's all that it means—the not-light when the heart breaks and the chest caves in, like a nest abandoned, blown open to the wind. Sometimes, it takes a life.

Antonio

A Hole in the Sky (Pt. 2)

WHEN MY UNCLE TONINO visited the States in May 1985, British me-
teorologists had just discovered a hole in the ozone layer above Ant-
arctica. During a Memorial Day picnic at Manasquan Beach, I obsessed
over widespread melanoma in Australia and blinded llamas in the
Andes. Blame CFCs and corporate malfeasance! Tonino, who worked
with legendary ad man Armando Testa, had not endured a ten-hour
flight from Rome to Newark to be harangued by an unemployed college
graduate and parlor Socialist.

"The sky has always had a hole in it," Tonino announced. "Once
we patched it with frescos. Now we use billboards." He poured himself
a Campari and soda and would not be contradicted. As my parents
and he recalled past outings at Ostia and Vasto, I lay on a checkered
blanket and pondered his words. Above me, skywriters and balloonists
promoted Coppertone and Snapple. Shortly later, much to Tonino's
delight, I began working at Timely Advertising, a small agency in
North Plainfield, New Jersey.

My boss Steve Pell inherited his name, his copper-colored hair,
and his impish sense of humor from a Polish Jewish grandfather. Stefan
Pellowski had fled Gdańsk in November 1920, after the city's ethnic
Germans had assumed control and renamed it Danzig. Hitler partly
justified his invasion of Poland to "liberate" this German colony. Steve
did not display lithographs of Gdańsk in his office. Instead the walls
were hung with matted prints of Campbell's soup cans and a gigantic
framed poster of the Marx Brothers smoking a hookah.

"These pictures remind me that life is vaudeville," Steve said.
"Ethnic identity is a joke." Steve smirked and waited to see how I
would react. He teased me because I insisted on calling myself Antonio.
This baffled him. Life was hard enough in America without wearing a

foreign name like an albatross around your neck. "Success is about passing," Steve said. "Why stand outside the Golden Door? Say the secret word, and America will let you in."

"What's the secret word?" I asked.

"Swordfish!" crowed Steve, alluding to a classic Marx Brothers bit from *Horse Feathers*. Groucho tries to gain admittance to a speakeasy, but Chico the doorman demands the password. "I give you three guesses," he says. "It's the name of the fish." Groucho strokes his chin. *Is it sturgeon?* No, a sturgeon is a doctor who cut you open when-a you sick. *Is it haddock?* No, that's what you take-a aspirin for. Finally, Harpo arrives, pulls a sword and a fish out of his trenchcoat, and enters the speakeasy.

"That's why Julius Henry Marx became Groucho," Steve explained. "That's why Stefan Pellowski became Steve Pell," He opened a large art book on his desk and showed me a silkscreen of a poker-faced man with hollow cheeks and frizzy white hair. "And that's why Andrej Varhola became Andy Warhol."

❧

Born in Pittsburgh, Pennsylvania, Andrej Varhola Jr. was the fourth child of working-class Lemko immigrants from Mikó (modern Miková), once located in Hungary but now part of northeastern Slovakia. Warhol's father, who came to America before World War I, worked in a coalmine.

The Varholas lived at 55 Beelen Street and later at 3252 Dawson Street in Pittsburgh's Oakland neighborhood. The devout family attended St. John Chrysostom Byzantine Catholic Church. Little Andrej wanted to be an icon painter. He loved the hallucinatory power of Byzantine art.

After his father died in an industrial accident, Andrej started collecting autographed cards of film stars and eventually studied commercial art at the Carnegie Institute of Technology. Moving to New York in the 1950s, he changed his name and freelanced for ad agencies. He specialized in whimsical drawings of shoes and colorful record album covers. When he discovered silkscreen printing, he applied his training and technique to national symbols and iconic movie stars.

Walter Benjamin wrote an essay about art in the age of mechanical reproduction. Andy Warhol made a fortune mass-producing multiple prints of Campbell's soup cans and Marilyn Monroe. To drive home his point, he called his studio "The Factory" and surrounded himself with celebrities, socialites, drag queens, and porn stars. Reporters and professor asked him what he thought of art.

"Art?" said Andy, his face a death mask of irony and ennui. "I don't believe I know the man."

Warhol laughed all the way to the bank, but posthumously he became the victim of the prank he had pulled. Twenty-five years after his death, the Velvet Underground sued the Andy Warhol Foundation for copyright infringement over a banana logo. A prominent lawyer joked that "the band's fifteen minutes of litigation would end in a peel."

Before dying in his sleep from a sudden postoperative cardiac arrhythmia, Warhol was working on a Last Supper cycle. He drew almost one hundred variations on this theme, "which indicates," the Guggenheim claims, with a breathtaking gift for stating the obvious, "an almost obsessive investment in the subject matter." Part of him remained that devout Ruthenian Catholic boy who longed to paint icons. He attended daily mass, volunteered at soup kitchens, and paid for his nephew Mark's seminary tuition.

Andrej Varhola is buried in St. John the Baptist Byzantine Catholic Cemetery in Bethel Park, Pennsylvania, near his parents. But the most beautiful statue of Andy Warhol stands neither in Pittsburgh nor Manhattan but in Bratislava, Slovakia. Above these monuments spans an infinite blue sky, seemingly without a hole. *Odpočívaj v pokoji.*

Rest in peace.

III

History, Open for Business

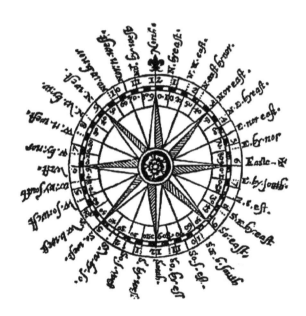

Andrei

Communism, the After-Christmas Sale

EVERY YEAR DURING FASHION WEEK in New York, somewhere along the streets of SoHo, curbside vendors hawk their wares on folding tables: oil-on-canvas art, handmade jewelry, leather goods, even Soviet propaganda T-shirts. What was once part of the Communist apparatus are now indulgences in the Church of Mammon. For $20, you too can walk around with Lenin's gleaming forehead proclaiming victory over capitalism or his bony finger pointing toward some distant imagined future.

Likely he never imagined this. But history is a business and a profitable one at that. Vintage propaganda posters go for a pretty penny these days on eBay. After all, they're colorful, well executed, and tinged with nostalgia for a time few actually remember or understand. And there lies the danger, or at least the irony. Are we condemned to repeat a tragic past or doomed to flaunt tasteless pop accessories in a farcical present?

Removed from their original context, printed in a language few on the streets of SoHo can read, these posters turned into T-shirts or pins or mouse pads have lost their intended value and serve simply as commodities, their meaning and attendant history buried and ignored under fashion and consumption. There are enough copies of copies and replicas by the hundreds for everyone to go to bed in hammer and sickle pajamas. In the end you can wear and wash them as much as you want, but they will never come clean. For many of us they are stained with too much to unremember.

☾

In St. Petersburg, Russia, I once met a man who sold such vintage posters of different sizes along with various other Communist paraphernalia.

Some posters drew my attention because they didn't seem to fit with the others. To put it simply, they were a bit lewd, even playfully sexy, though the slogans, like all the others, pretended to glorify the workers and the party. I asked the store owner if they were real. Deeply offended, he launched into a tirade about the risks of producing something of that nature only three decades ago. "You could go to jail for this!" he exclaimed. I knew that, but I very much wanted history to have a funny bone. That is the premise of Milan Kundera's *The Joke*, a satire on all kitsch: Christian, nationalist, and Communist. History laughs at our expense.

How many of those who pony up the $20 for a *Workers, Unite!* T-shirt are aware of the millions who suffered under the pretty glare of those colors? How many would still wear those posters (even as a fashion statement) if they only knew how much the truth still bites at our heels? But that is part of the problem. By turning history into a half-off special on street corners and inside pop-up boutiques, we have stripped it of its power to teach, of its ability to inform our actions. We no longer hold up ideals because they are too big to understand within the frame of a T-shirt or baseball cap or Che Guevara lapel pin.

Henry Giroux, in his 2013 essay *The Violence of Organized Forgetting*, describes the condition we find ourselves in this way: "Large social movements fragmented into isolated pockets of resistance mostly organized around a form of identity politics." In other words, social movements increasingly take on the guise of actions based on self-interest that serve specialized interest groups. We now support causes, so many causes that our ability for critical thought, for questioning and engagement, is fractured and reduced to sloganeering and flag waving from the sidelines. We support causes because they supply us with images, sound bites, and tie-in products. We can buy our moral high ground and wear it as a wristband or proclaim our righteousness on bumper stickers. Subsequently we join this or that 5K walk or benefit and check off our charitable contributions. We create inspirational Internet memes that take words and images out of context and employ them for purposes they were never intended. Facing the glare of the screen we chuckle at how aptly they capture the futility of the moment, and we move on to the next frame, the next easy smirk.

And when we get bored or tired, when the *cause du jour* trips in the dust because another celebrity spokesperson went to rehab, when too many T-shirts are left over from yet another human rights benefit concert and too many embroidered hats are shipped by the kilo to Third World countries, a sun-wrinkled old man walks around in the desert with *I Voted for Ryan* printed on his chest. Meanwhile, history keeps thumbing its nose and walks right on by as we make plans for the weekend, willfully forgetful of our own complicity.

One Kiss, for the Revolution

A whole life spent with the saints at your back. One day you swap your wings, stand naked before the blindfolded statue of another ghost town on the heels of the plow. Nothing to your name but a name. You get in line with the rest of them and the week's last dollar in your hand. There's beer and blues in the salty air of twilight, smoke on the tar-papered walls, the cheap, simple passion on the precipice of some need, one kiss, for the revolution.

☾

You stay up all night wondering how it ended up like this. Your shoulders feathered by the rain, the sheer curtain you must push aside to reach the other side. Imperfect as ever. From the wreckage a face of the past of the newly combed dirt of the pallid morning blooming from balconies. Spring's rain weeps from your eyes and there she is, a stranger until that moment, with the sway of her hair, the grieving waist, the one thing she has to give, one kiss, for the revolution.

☾

In the aged store window your words crowd uncertain of themselves onto the tip of speech. The hour is otherwise silent and somber, warmed by the fire tearing through darkness. When you put your nose to the glass the fog blurs the impoverished streets. The dignity of their despair clings to every brick that hasn't crumbled, every candle lit inside the kitchens of the poor as they pray for the less fortunate. They list name after name and it takes them a long time to finish. And before bed with open arms they lean over the beds of their fathers, of their children, not with misery on their breath, not with suffocating fear. Just one kiss, for the revolution.

Open for Business

One-legged beggars broken at the feet of statues; open for business. In their halter tops and skinny jeans the girls walk by, spent shells of the sexual revolution. They are talking strategy. Their conversations scripted and efficient because all of the good parts are already taken. The real message comes in the twenty-fifth frame when the shimmy of a skirt in full bloom reminds me of the projects. Stoop sitting on summer nights with Nelu when I spent hours staring at the sky wishing I could stare at the sky somewhere else. He could blow smoke rings that swallowed up the moon. He was twelve. Lately I wonder if the revolution really did come true. Maybe we are all dead. Coke bottle Molotovs and flower launchers in each hand as we march over rough blossoms of cracked asphalt, past the church with revolving doors. A new street rigged with electric lanterns for that Old World appeal. The Old World where I am an aching tooth that I cannot shake loose and the sunrise is a lemon sugared over because it makes things easier to swallow. We use lollipops to wipe away tears. We leave our toy machine guns in the dirt then climb into bed dreaming smoke rings under a different sky.

Imperial Song

How do you settle debts with the dead and missing? I looked for them through the glass hoping for a different answer. The note I wedged in the door is certain to be smudged by the rain.

Meanwhile the street sweeper outside went about the business of sweeping. At church, the faithful got down on broken knees and hid their eyes. A howl was born in the most remote valleys and mountains. If anyone heard, they pretended that it was only a matter of time.

I walked back to my apartment staring into many dilated pupils. My whispers were not enough to stop any of them. And my breaths were not enough to be anything more than whispers. And when the sky finally dared to turn into a dove I heard someone take a shot at the sky then burst into an imperial song.

I cried in silence; cried without tears because they would never be enough. Out on the balconies, waving its ragged and soiled undergarments, the future put on a show with a second-rate cast and a skeleton script. Much of it was blacked out; even our names.

Antonio

The Last Mirage (Pt. 1)

AMID THE SAND AND HAZE OF NEVADA wavers the last mirage of Europe. In Las Vegas, history truly is "open for business." The Strip's most popular luxury hotels mock and exploit European civilization. Caesar's Palace resurrects the glory that was Rome so that polo-shirted Trimalchios can flaunt their cash. The Monte Carlo, inspired by the Principality of Monaco's Place du Casino, recreates the Belle Époque. Retirees send their children iPhone photos of chandelier domes, marble floors, neoclassical arches, ornate fountains, and gaslit promenades.

European intellectuals journey to Las Vegas to study this spectacle. More often than not, they are seduced by it. Like Professor Rath in *The Blue Angel*, Jean Baudrillard utterly succumbed to "the great whore on the other side of the desert." Wearing a gold lamé suit with mirrored lapels, the French philosopher and sociologist read his avant-garde poetry to the boozy regulars at Whiskey Pete's, a second-rate casino near the state line. When Walter Benjamin's Angel of History plays the slot machines, the house always wins.

Postmodernism has replaced the European city, with its parliaments and cathedrals framing the plaza, with the American shopping mall. "In the historical era," notes the social philosopher William Irwin Thompson in *The American Replacement of Nature: The Everyday Acts and Outrageous Evolution of Economic Life* (1991), "monumental art, with its great buildings and heroes on horseback impressed the citizen with civilization; but now in our post-historic condition, history is not a text, but a quote from old movies in a theme-park ride."

This catastrophic transformation harbingers an emerging global culture. Like a catalytic enzyme, Thompson predicts, America will dissolve and synthesize "all the traditional cultures of the world, be they Asiatic, Islamic, or European." As an Old World humanist, I am not optimistic about the outcome, but Thompson makes a good point: "The classical stage set of the old European ruling class had to be seen from one angle only to maintain the illusion of depth." Impossible in a post-Western world of multiple perspectives, but I still crave *trompe-l'œil.* So do most Italians.

An addiction to spectacle and illusion, claimed Luigi Barzini, is our defining vice. It might even be genetic, judging from my family on both sides of the Atlantic. When life overwhelms me in Rome, I seek asylum in the Musei Vaticani or the Teatro dell' Opera. My cousin Tony, a harried police dispatcher from Syracuse, New York, books a suite at the Venetian Las Vegas. The Venetian replicates the Rialto Bridge and St. Mark's Campanile and includes an artificial lagoon. Lolling in gondolas, call girls in taffeta pretend to be courtesans. "Better than the real thing," Tony says and winks.

He should know. Tony's branch of the family comes from Veneto, not Abruzzo. Back in the thirteenth century, his cloth-merchant ancestors traveled to Cathay with Niccolò and Maffeo Polo and returned seventeen years later with Mongolian wives. For this reason, Tony and his three brothers look Chinese. They frequently visit and Skype with relatives. I've never gotten farther than Padua.

"Vegas might be Sin City," Tony says, "but so was Venice. It was a floating crap game." He is right, of course. During the eighteenth century, La Serenissima profited from gambling and prostitution and trafficked in illusions. Her squares swarmed with poets and parasites, barbers and moneylenders, pimps and whores, virtuosos, ballerinas, castrati, and croupiers. All made their living out of pleasure and luxury. Time sped in a round of shows and concerts. Life itself passed like a play at some fête.

Venice was called the City of Masks. Because carnival lasted six months, people felt obliged to go out in costume. Every day was a masquerade, an intrigue, an assignation. A proverb captures this reckless hedonism: "*Messetta, bassetta e donnetta.*" In the morning a little mass, in the afternoon a little party, in the evening a little lady. Amid such giddiness and frivolity, everything durable was a source of ennui.

Still, Venice was glorious in her slow decline, a consumptive perishing in satin sheets. Out of a veil of tenderest blue, soft as mist, cradled in a translucent vapor, the dying Queen of the Sea rose like a dream of rose and marble. Air and water wove for her a robe and shroud of fantasy. Opal and mother-of-pearl, coral, ivory, and silver were wedded in a riot of soft pink, palest violet, and lucent grey. Over everything shone a wonderful light, more enchanting than any Tiepolo. It bathed the city's domes, cupolas, and towers in an exquisite brightness, displaying its spires and pinnacles in a trellised daintiness more like lace than stone.

When the Republic fell in 1797, Venice became a museum, an outdoor salon for poets, lovers, art historians, and exiles. A discontented backwater under the Hapsburgs, the city failed to regain its status after joining the Kingdom of Italy in 1866. "When Venice was a Republic," lamented diplomat Daniele Varé, "our word was law all down the Adriatic. Now every petty southern Slav can defy us with impunity!" Not to mention every petty Roman bureaucrat. Concluding the city was a money sink, the new national government denied it financial aid, setting the stage for its final disintegration.

Few objected. Committed to progress, liberal politicians thought that Venice should sink. So did radical artists. Filippo Tommaso Marinetti, the Futurist poet, called La Serenissima "a city of dead fish and decaying houses, inhabited by a race of waiters and touts." Modern Italy, he said, should be like the United States, a mighty world power full of cement houses, huge music halls, and trains that ran on time. America, for its part, considered Venice a theme park. When Frederick Law Olmstead designed the 1893 Chicago World's Fair, he based the Grand Basin with its lagoons and gondolas on the Grand Canal.

Venice's humiliation was symptomatic. The scientific, industrial, and political revolutions of the nineteenth century, culminating in America's ascendance, had brought Europe material prosperity but cultural desolation. When art and philosophy failed to create a bulwark against modernity, the politics of resentment paved the way for the catastrophes of the next century.

Myths of the nationalistic past lead to Fascism. Visions of the utopian future lead to Communism. Both totalitarian ideologies utterly destroyed a continent. Although Western Europe has recovered physically, it has become an ornate but empty shell, preserved for tourists and speculators. Scavenging gulls have picked clean the actual conch.

Andrei

Bad Habits of Old Women

We took one of those on-the-hour bus tours where you could watch from a distance the fires light up each circle of hell. All history is political, explained our resident expert, sweeping his hand over Chairman Mao smiling down at us from a vintage poster in someone's otherwise empty bedroom. And Stalin, that jokester in his new bohemian rags, was down at the park blowing up balloons for the little children. He thinks positive thoughts and doesn't cry for the dead because everything happens for a reason. At night he cannot fall asleep without a warm glass of milk.

Truly, it was nothing out of the ordinary—the woman wearing a secondhand wedding dress as a statement about metaphysics—my grandmother muttering *Go fuck yourselves* as we passed the busy storefront of another decade. Typical end-of-century nonsense. Some of us got out for souvenirs anyway. Cheap forgeries and replicas. Everything carried a hidden message of some sort. I bought a green army hat with an emblem spit-shined to a blinding yellow. The same kind I wore in a photograph in another country while Grandmother pushed back the whiskey listened to the radio and repeated her favorite phrase.

First Sign of Promise

Snow steadies itself parallel to the eye.
Stillness points a finger back at us.

Unbearable cold is a good time for the civilized to confess, but the things of this earth of any importance have been reduced to summaries of lovemaking and awkward family dinners—

outside, the year's first snow falls on eyelashes and the neighborhood square. It buries all of our victories, the left over shriveled wreaths no one dares to call tasteless—

and anyway, even if we wanted to, what would it accomplish? In this labyrinth of the living there simply aren't enough words to last us through the endless night and then beyond into the dance. So we ration out breath and language, talk only of permitted signs, how if it keeps snowing much longer we won't have anything left to say.

Vicious Cycle

In an act of petty burglary someone ripped off a corner of the republic and placed it underneath his tongue like the body of Christ. And with that he was content to go without food or water, modern luxuries, anything that would slow him down. My son, *you cannot live as a common thief and expect forgiveness—you must return what you took without asking,* said a priest before crossing himself and chewing on a large chunk of bread. The man spit out the torn edge and realized that it no longer fit in its place, swollen with the blood he'd been forced to swallow just so he wouldn't choke. He held it in his hand, unable to throw it away. Useless now even as charity.

Antonio

The Last Mirage (Pt. 2)

A PROCESSION OF THREE GONDOLAS bears an empty coffin from Venice's Piazzale Roma train station, down the Grand Canal to the Rialto Bridge. Drummers beat a death march. Pallbearers lift the fuchsia casket onto dry land and, followed by black-clad mourners, deposit it at Palazzo Cavalli. Venessia, a grassroots organization, has organized this mock funeral to shame the city council. Speaking through a megaphone, Stefano Soffiato, the group's founder and leader, reads the bills of mortality.

Sky-high rents and exorbitant property prices, fueled by investors and corporations eager to exploit Venice's art and history, have caused a mass exodus to towns on the mainland. Andrea Morelli, whose family pharmacy has operated near the Rialto Bridge since the sixteenth century, has installed an electronic ticker to record the daily population decline. According to the census, the number of permanent residents has sunk below 58,500. One in four is over sixty-four years old. The city, warns the registrar, could be devoid of full-time, native-born inhabitants as early as 2030.

"If Venetians continue to leave Venice," Soffiato shouts, "Venice will disappear and all that will remain is a Disneyland!" This prospect delights most travel agents.

Each year, twenty million tourists flood Venice—a twentyfold increase since 1950, when the city's population was 175,000. Budget flights and cheap package deals have put Venice within reach of more people than ever before. Around 55,000 day trippers arrive every morning. Surging through the narrow alleyways and squares, they swamp the city, making ordinary business impossible. Family stores are forced to operate as tourist shops, selling imitation carnivals masks and Murano glass. Restaurants and hotels fare worse. Most tourists bring a bag lunch. Almost none stay the night. Neither the Wi-Fi in Florian's Coffee House nor the flat-screen TVs at the Hotel Danieli can entice them. Before sunset, the human tide reverses and by early evening, Venice is a ghost town.

Tourism has overwhelmed the local economy. Since 2007, the number of historic buildings converted into bed and breakfasts has gone up over 1,000 percent. A bed and breakfast is on virtually every corner, while new hotels open literally every day. Every fall, Venice hosts a prestigious international film festival but for the rest of the year makes do with one commercial movie house. Alilaguna, the water transport company, buys its vaporettos from Greece because nobody builds them locally. Banks, once a cornerstone of the Venetian economy, have disappeared. When Assicurazioni Generali, Italy's largest insurance company (whose logo features the Lion of St. Mark), closed its doors, one thousand white-collar workers lost their jobs.

The only gainfully employed are oceanographers and engineers from the University of Padua, who grimly measure the city's rising tides and crumbling foundations. Venice is sinking five times faster than anticipated in 2001, thanks to global warming. But the more immediate environmental threat is ship traffic. More than 650 cruise ships visit each year, six a day at the height of tourist season. They enter and leave via the Giudecca Canal, which skirts the Grand Canal and separates the island of Giudecca from Venice proper. Some ships are gargantuan. The MSC *Divina*, three times the size of the Titanic, dwarfs the Basilica of Santa Maria, built to celebrate Venice's delivery from the plague.

Such super cruisers, UNESCO reports, damage the city's fragile infrastructure. Their wakes erode the foundations of buildings. Their engine oil pollutes the lagoon and creates a miasma of stench. Their height ruins the skyline and obscures monuments. Even so, the city council dares not regulate traffic. Each ship generates revenue from docking fees and from food, water, and supplies purchased from local contractors. The cruise industry also employs an estimated three thousand Venetians, a fact often repeated in corporate literature and promoted at the lavish Festa del Porto held at the end of October.

The real carnival, however, is the orgy of advertising. To raise money for desperately needed restoration and preservation projects, the cash-strapped city council must resort to corporate sponsorship. The Palazzo Ducale, once the seat of the world's oldest and longest continuing republic, is defaced by billboards for Coca-Cola, Dolce & Gabbana, Moët, and Rolex. Bulgari has transformed the Bridge of Sighs into the Bridge of Signs. Art historians and museum directors protest. After the great flood of 1966, when Venice was in a much worse state and Italy a much poorer country, no one contemplated using such crass methods to raise funds. An alternative must be found, otherwise Venice is doomed to be covered in ads for the rest of its life. Its landmarks require constant care due to their great age and the city's environmental fragility.

"If purists want to see a building," retorts Mayor Giorgio Assoni, "they should go home and look at a picture of it in a book." His attitude dismays not only native residents but also migrant workers from Albania, Bulgaria, Croatia, Romania, Serbia, and Slovenia, who consider Venice their second home. Once part of the Austro-Hungarian Empire, Venice maintains commercial ties with Vienna, Trieste, and Dubrovnik, which supply its hotels and resorts with summer help. Many Slavs have married Venetians. They speak the local dialect and cook local delicacies. But perhaps the most devoted foreign residents are the expatriates from St. Petersburg, Russia, Venice's sister city, who are appalled to see the Queen of the Adriatic become a Potemkin village.

"It's a grotesque tragedy worthy of Gogol," says a lecturer at the Ca' Foscari Center for Advanced Studies on Russian Culture and Arts, who prefers to remain anonymous after being reprimanded for denouncing the university for awarding an honorary fellowship to Vladimir Medinsky, Russia's Minister of Culture. Medinsky, a notorious Putin hack, had dismissed the Russian program curator at the Venice Biennale, Grigory Revzin, just two months before its opening. "When Napoleon conquered Venice, he razed a palazzo to build a ballroom. He also plundered galleries and churches and stole the Basilica of San Marco's four bronze horses for the Arc de Triomphe du Carrousel. Venice survived such atrocities, but I'm not sure it will survive plastic gondolas."

At Harry's Bar—once Ernest Hemingway's favorite watering hole, now a franchise of Cipriani S.A., which owns and operates luxury clubs and restaurants around the world—the dwindling regulars sip Bellini cocktails and commiserate about the future. The more imaginative envision apocalyptical scenarios of the last "real Venetians" caged on show in the Piazza San Marco like so many pandas, unable to breed or chew *bigoli*, or of wrought-iron gates clanging shut at night after straggling shoppers, their passes expired, exit an open-air mall cum museum. Others predict that Venice will disappear in a century, with only the Campanile and the domes of the Salute rising above the water. Perhaps then enterprising Americans will organize scuba diving tours. For now, the Queen of the Adriatic shimmers on the lagoon, a fading mirage.

IV

An Autopsy of Belief

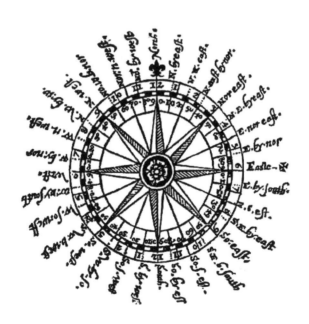

Andrei

Pray Daily: Use Words If You Must

I COME BACK TIME AND AGAIN to the words above, seen in passing on a roadside sign outside an upstate New York church. Supposedly, they come from Francis of Assisi. Umbria's gentle hills are a world away from the hardscrabble terrain of the Southern Tier, but Francis's words still haunt me. Not because he was a saint but because he was a poet. A troubadour who decided to court Lady Poverty, he wrote "The Canticle of the Sun," the first major poem in the Italian vernacular. Maybe that is why Francis puzzles me. Pray, if not with words, then with what? And for what?

If I shared Francis's faith, I might better understand what he was saying. But as someone who from childhood has had a tortured relationship with the Romanian Orthodox Church—the gloomy bearded priests, the hollow-eyed saints and guttering candle, interminable, suffocating services, all of it shrouded in incense—I can conceive of prayer only in the most secular sense: as a plea, a request, a desire, a hope. Can the faithless pray in the name of passion?

The German lyric poet Rilke spent a lifetime trying to answer this question. Raised in an atmosphere of hothouse piety, he rejected God and became the ultimate Prodigal Son. While his family and friends in *fin de siècle* Prague found meaning and identity in organized religion or conventional morality, Rilke found his in the search for impressions and the hope that these could be turned into poetry. For him, art was faith and faith was art.

"Rilke's mystical, philosophical poems," said W. H. Auden, "work through imagery. He expresses ideas with physical rather than intellectual symbols. While Shakespeare, for example, thought of the non-human world in terms of the human, Rilke thinks of the human in terms of the non-human, of what he calls Things (*Dinge*)."

For a lapsed Orthodox Christian such as myself, Auden's insight resonates deeply. Religion always seeks to embody its ideals—whether through a direct incarnation (prophets, saviors, etc.) or physical representation, such as icons and statues. Even Judaism and Islam, which officially forbid such representation, are rich in patterns and symbols. It is almost impossible then to separate prayer from an image, an object toward which it is directed. We must pray then in images, in an imagined ideal version of the canon.

Yet, much like any ideal, God is ultimately unknowable, only approachable, a sort of pursuit if you will. He is not understandable in and of himself except through his creations: without those things we would lack the necessary tools to navigate toward him. Then, the act of creation on his part can be considered a deliberate attempt to be understood, since it is only through our relationship to things and to one another that we *come to know* (both the world around us and ourselves). It would mean then that prayer of any sort is kind of a halfway meeting point, a joint effort between man and God toward *becoming* or understanding.

Are we not Godlike then in the simplest way, since we must literally and figuratively create and mediate with the world to understand it? Like rail workers on an infinite train line, we lay down tracks so that we might remember our way back to some origins but also so that we might move forward toward the unknowable, hoping someone or something will lend us a hand.

Such a dynamic relationship demands that we make sense of the role of words, images, and imagination in this journey. Because poetry plays with all these things, it has the ability to reveal and preserve the mystery behind the ordinary. But isn't that also the role of dogma, to separate the knowable from the unknowable and to dare imagination to bridge the gap? Whether we listen to the words of the mass or Rilke's *Book of Hours*, we are compelled to ask: "What does this mean? Why does it make me feel this way?" In a sense, poetry is a call to an authority within and outside us, a seeking for a resolution or explanation beyond words.

Interpreted as strict orthodoxy, this is exactly the role of prayer. It translates the image into the language that evokes it and forces the mind to understand it. The more "new" that language and the more startling the images, the more it stands a chance of simultaneously calling attention to some established doctrine but also of moving away from it—hence the possibility of some form of transcendence being achieved through the poetic impulse.

Therein lies the beauty of poetry and the danger. Utterly transcendent, it separates the secular from the sacred. No wonder totalitarian regimes fear the poet more than any other artist. Icons of St. Basil can become models for posters of Lenin, Easter processions can be converted into May Day parades, but the Ministry of Propaganda cannot exploit an unfathomable poem. The greatest poets have found a way to pray on their own, subverting dogma and empowering outcasts to articulate and imagine what is possible. "The limits of your language are the limits of your world," said Ludwig Wittgenstein. Poetry pushes those limits and teaches us to desire freely, to dare to hope. With all respect to five centuries of Romanian patriarchs, this for me is *dreapta credinţă*, true belief, and so I offer this prayer:

TO EASTERN EUROPEAN POETS

love-roughened, timeless,

splinters caught in a derelict rain
saints of the catastrophe cathedral
smoking cigarettes
still standing at the end of
yet another miserable decade

their fire burning poetry on book covers.

When the Oil Burns Low

Le silence éternal de ces espaces infinis m'effraie.
—Pascal

It could've been that we were too tired to go any farther. Someone clutching Mary wrapped around his neck was mumbling and no one needed to ask why. It could've been a prayer. We didn't ask. The soft light of late summer dusk seemed to go on forever, spun out of innocence and child's breath and centuries of dinner getting cold upon the table. The dark fell like a web, pooled in the corners, rubbed its face into the dirt that gathered at our feet. We were alone, haunted by the silence. We wore the blood of our fears, we wore the dim marquee of lineage, the messy paint over a crippled shack. To keep the young from weeping we took turns making small animal sounds. We gave them the body of Mary for a bright-colored toy. We even sent them out into the open to cross bridges and waters, to come back from the ocean with a new love of the bluest sky and their own supply of abandoned dreams. Something like mirrors, open doors to the infinite, and far away the light of one candle making frightening faces.

The City of Logical Conclusions

Men were out in the streets pulling at the loaded wagon of history. Flowers were growing from eye sockets, mouths were all root and clay. I cleared my throat and turned a blind eye to the colonnade of dying birch trees. There were many other warnings of the impassable road, the bad weather. A flood of humanity downtrodden passing by in the other direction.

◖

But what demoralized man doesn't count on his luck just one more time? Pray with more virtue than those who prostrate themselves daily? I cleared my throat again and stood bottle in hand propping up the wheel. The horses were unhitched, the stone opera house was an abandoned backdrop—a play unfolding on the main stage already snagged in the cobwebs of memory.

◖

While the soul's immensity was being measured in a span of loneliness, everyone waited for the clock to tumble out of destiny. I managed to lift myself up long enough to see the last beautiful shimmer, the far off air shivering in heat and particles of dust. And then I couldn't clear my throat any more. I smelled lilac and I closed my eyes.

A Rough Angelology

We teeter on the knife-edge light from one day to the next, an avalanche of angels falling on temples and altars—pine rubbed, weatherproof. We stay where we are, overgrown with shock. The way ruins stand in time over bloodrivers and weddings, witness to parts, record of stone soggy with pleasure.

ℭ

To see better whole branches are punched out of the sky, filled in with space, the broken joints of winter and clouds. The birds haven't flown to better lands, are still in the frozen trees. Beyond our help. As we are beyond theirs.

ℭ

So we move now only as lumps in the throat, swallowed the memory of being found hung by our necks, shoulder-bound and vulnerable—as anything conceived to be admired.

Antonio

Duino Elegies (Pt. 1)

RAINER MARIA RILKE was the last Western poet to communicate with angels. Highly strung, he was an antenna picking up signals from the great beyond. The first broadcast occurred in January 1912. At the time, Rilke was living at Duino Castle, a fourteenth-century fort on the steep cliffs overlooking the Gulf of Trieste, where the exiled Dante Alighieri worked on the *Divine Comedy*. For four months, Rilke had been translating Dante's *Vita Nuova* with his hostess, Princess Marie von Thurn und Taxis, whose husband's ancestors founded the German imperial postal service. No wonder fate decided to deliver a message.

Rilke had received a distressing letter that demanded an immediate reply. Anxious, he walked out to the battlements and climbed down a narrow path along the cliffs to the castle's bastions. As he paced along the shore, brooding about the letter, the weather turned. The waves pounded. The wind roared. From the gathering storm, a voice howled in German: "*Wer, wenn ich schriee, hörte mich denn aus der Engel Ordnungen?*" Who, if I cried out, would hear me among the angelic orders? Rilke took out his notebook, which he always carried with him, and wrote down what would become the first line of the *Duino Elegies*, a collection of ten mystical poems, often considered Rilke's masterpiece.

Rilke was convinced an angel had spoken to him. Princess Marie smiled. Her pet poet was too ethereal for this world, which was why she called him *Dottore Serafico*. Rilke, however, became obsessed. The following winter, he lived in Andalusia. Ravished by the Alhambra, consumed by the Koran, he studied Islamic angelology.

According to Moslem tradition, angels are intangible beings, who lack or have renounced free will. Their sole purpose is to serve God. Being made of light, they can assume almost any form and can travel the length of the entire universe faster than thought. God's messengers, angels pass between heaven and earth and communicate to humans. Each has a sacred task.

Azrael (whose name means "Whom God Helps") appears to the dying to separate them from their mortal remains. Unlike the Grim Reaper, Azrael does not wear a cowl of sackcloth but a robe of fire, each tongue of flame corresponding to the earth's human inhabitants. At the end of time, he will record and erase in a large book the names of men at birth and death, respectively. When this task is done, he and the universe will disappear in a ball of fire. Based on hints from his poems and letters, Rilke seems to have believed that this was the angel who had contacted him at Duino Castle. If this is true, Azrael's voice seared his heart.

"Every angel is terrible," Rilke declared. Pouring over apocryphal scriptures and discarded legends, he had discovered a devastating secret. Neither angels nor devils care about humanity. They care only about God. Humanity, after all, had caused the pointless war between them. Once upon a time, they were all Sons of Light, blissfully obedient to God. When God created humans, however, He decided to endow them with free will, a gift denied to every other creature. The Sons of Light thought that this was a bad idea, but Michael advised his brothers to go along. Lucifer, however, begged God to reconsider. "Mark my words!" he said. "These ungrateful apes will turn on you!"

But God insisted. Worse, He demanded that the Sons of Light pledge their love and loyalty to humans, a violation of their sacred oath of exclusive allegiance to God. Lucifer balked. He adored God's perfection and would accept nothing less. He refused to equate a creature with the Creator. At that moment, to the horror of the Sons of Light, Lucifer fell from heaven, dragging half the angelic hosts with him. Ever since, he and his minions have enticed humans to commit evil, not out of spite but conviction. They gather evidence to prove that God made a terrible mistake, hoping the Old Man will recognize His error and reconcile with Lucifer.

The twentieth century would win their case.

Andrei

Between Gods

After all those years twisting at the rope of jealousy, dwelling on the sins of others; we get ahead of ourselves, we get lost on purpose. And because we suffer through it, we are as they say, blameless, barely a moment past grace—banished from discussing the present because it is already smoldering inside the ruins of the past. Inside violent, turbulent waters...

afterward we try to do the impossible, balance at the tender midpoint. But we aren't young anymore and neither is anyone else who is old enough to remember. This is how we tip to the side of least resistance, the religion of old age. Where before there were gaps in logic now everything, in the proper light, has a place and a purpose. *Proper* meaning naked, vulnerable, circumstantial...

a tender icon, oil on pine, watching over long nights wasted with a glass and cigarette at the mouth. And now, who can recall the exact day when it all went horribly wrong? We lost track of the hour and the number, the many black and white judgments it took before we became numb to the customary kiss.

Fortunately some things will remain simply unaccounted for. Stubborn even in the hands of death. For what can fit between us and the gods we've tied around our necks? Not even a name. Not even blood.

The Candle Is Out; No Matches

In the cupboard of the lost St. Anthony is down on his knees among the chipped mugs and the dull dirty knives. His pockets are crammed with what isn't there. Even that they want to take away. Obliterate traces. And in that cruel humility born out of being born someone climbs upon the bent-back shouting with a fool's conviction. Waving an arm and a fist. You know him, I presume? Crumbs for your thoughts then. The clatter of rain for your thoughts. Gather them into an offering—into a voice—

I'll tell you mine—I am picturing grass—one blade among thousands. On a mountain. The noise of many moving among us. How the mind becomes silent in an empty field sown with the tongues of the blameless. They are occupied looking for stones. No one hears anymore the ones who pray just to be heard. To talk to someone in their loneliness as plain as you and I. St. Anthony is there too, feeling the way on his knees. His eyes are closed. There are walls to guide him and the darkness to see by. He is not looking for stones. He touches the place where the stone used to be and imagines the sound of its dying wish. There is ache and hunger crammed into that silence. Into each hollow. So much that he's barely moved an inch; he's still there listening.

Arrival of the Invitation; Inconclusive Directions

One: Wear the cloak of the vague when you go out for the night. Carry nothing in your pockets that you wouldn't mind tossing to the side of the road. Better yet, tear out your pockets. Get a tight grip on darkness with both of your fists. Let it pull you along, whispering past silhouettes of churches and trees, their likeness codified into a shiver.

Two: When you come to the fork in the road you will think of salvation. Everyone does. A monotonous carnival of three to four choices. Out of all of them choose to turn back around; have the strength not to go any farther.

Three: Back at the house whoever is waiting for you at dawn with folded arms and a scowl wants to be reassured. But you've got nothing in your pockets, nothing to show where you've been all this time.

Four: Be assured only that everything has outlived your absence. Everything is contingent upon your absence. Even you, seduced as you are by arbitrary freedoms. Vague hope, dark attic emptier than glory. Emptier still than this indefinite present you huddle over, palms around the rickety flame.

Antonio

Duino Elegies (Pt. 2)

CANNONS MUFFLED THE CELESTIAL CHOIR. On June 10, 1915, an Italian cruiser bombarded Trieste, supposedly to secure the Gulf of Panzano against Monfalcone, a strategic Austrian port to the north. The attack, however, was only a feint. The real Monfalcone campaign would be launched from another quarter across the Isonzo delta. Regardless, Duino Castle was blown to bits and set on fire.

On November 26, Rilke was drafted into the Austro-Hungarian army. Basic training nearly killed the forty-year-old poet. Never robust, he endured terrible pain. He also suffered flashbacks to his nightmare years in the Linz Military Academy. Alarmed, Hugo von Hoffmansthal and Stefan Zweig petitioned to have him transferred to the Vienna War Archives, where he toiled from the end of January to June of 1916. Despite this preferential treatment, Rilke was utterly traumatized and could not write. After the war, he moved to Switzerland, where a new patron, Werner Reinhart, bought and renovated the Château de Muzot, near Sierre. Beginning in 1921, Rilke lived here, rent-free, and gradually recovered his health and sanity.

At the poet's request, Muzot had no electricity. Rilke preferred to read by candlelight. Candles, he explained, aided meditation. Light bulbs killed contemplation. For Rilke, they represented "the false radiance of modernity." The war had nearly destroyed Old Europe, but the postwar boom, Rilke believed, debased what had survived. Paris was an anthill of traffic, London a peep show of commerce. Even Geneva had become "a conspiracy of hotels," designed to entice wealthy Americans, who were cheerfully remaking the world in their own image. Nothing could stop them. Like Nietzsche, Rilke believed Western religion was bankrupt. Christianity, "that fruit sucked dry," was particularly barren in America, where prohibitionists and evangelicals "keep brewing with the same shreds of tea that have steeped now for two millennia." When the Madman in *Thus Spoke Zarathustra* enters the bustling marketplace, he announces the death of God. When Americans surveyed the same scene, they proclaimed the Gospel of Progress.

In this futuristic nightmare of rampant technology and soulless materialism, poetry was God's final hiding place. Its resonance, however, depended on silence. What silence was possible in a world poised on the brink of mass broadcasting? But before Marconi's radio permanently replaced Dante's music of the spheres, Rilke received one last high-frequency transmission from the astral plane.

On February 2, 1922, after ten years of silence, the angels began dictating again. Rilke wrote like a man possessed. "It was an indescribable storm," he later said, "a mental and spiritual hurricane (as in those days of Duino). Every fiber, every tissue in me cracked—eating was never to be thought of. God knows what nourished me." Three weeks later, he had completed not only the *Duino Elegies* but the *Sonnets to Orpheus*. The strain wrecked his health. He became so weak that he was forced to move to the Valmont Sanatorium on Lake Geneva, where doctors discovered he had contracted leukemia.

With treatment, Rilke was allowed to return to his hermitage at Muzot. One day, he was visited by Nimet Eloui, the kohl-eyed daughter of the First Chamberlain to Sultan Hussein of Egypt, whom Rilke had met on the terrace of the Hotel Savoy at Lausanne. To honor this great beauty, he gathered some roses from his garden. While doing so, he pricked his left hand on a thorn. The small wound festered until his entire arm was swollen. The infection spread to his right arm and ulcerated his lips and tongue. As his condition worsened, he was transported back to Valmont, where he died in the arms of his doctor on December 29, 1926. His eyes were wide open, staring at the sky. If the heavens wept, nobody heard. Twenty years later, Rilke's spirit guide—Azrael the fiery Al-Death, the Scribe of Judgment—burned the world to ashes.

After Auschwitz and Hiroshima, the angels abandoned creation. That, anyway, is the current myth of Western civilization. If it is true, we have no one to blame but ourselves. As Azrael explained to Rilke, angels do not guard us out of love for humanity but obedience to God. When human beings act as if they have killed God, angels are no longer obliged to protect us. They are quite happy to leave us to our devils. "Some eighty years after Rilke's death," says critic Lee Siegel, "we live in modernism's plastic aftermath. Once, the modernists deployed dark energies of nihilism and unreason against the hated bourgeoisie; now those same energies galvanize a commercial civilization that is voraciously accommodating to nihilism and unreason."

True poetry, Rilke would have said, cannot survive such conditions. But old habits die hard. Western poets still serenade angels, even while doubting their existence, fully knowing that if these cruel messengers took one step down toward them from behind the stars, their hearts would explode. When the sky rages, however, these faithless poets do not hear the crackle of lightning. Only the static of a long-dead radio.

V

The Cunning of Reason

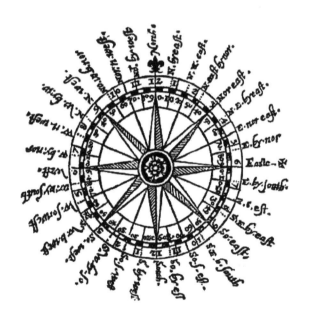

Andrei

Peddling Myth

> The spectacle in general, as the concrete inversion of life, is the
> autonomous movement of the non-living.
> —Guy Debord, *The Society of the Spectacle*

SIMPLY MENTION ROMANIA, and most Westerners will fantasize about
Dracula. It's not their fault, really, nor is it ill-intentioned. It is a Pav-
lovian tic conditioned by 130 years of Gothic novels and the auto-
matic video loop projected from Universal Studios' celluloid crypt.
This blood-and-sepia footage includes a number of typically spooky
soundtracks programmed to elicit a gasp or, at the very least, a titter.
Pure camp, of course, but it has turned Romania into the land of vampires, of myth easily debunked but not as easily erased from popular
consciousness.

Every year thousands of tourists from inside and outside Romania
travel to the craggy region of Brașov to visit *Castelul Bran*, the castle
of the historical "Dracula," or Vlad III, Prince of Wallachia and scion
of the House of Drăculești. Here (as in the many souvenir shops of
central Bucharest and duty-free counters at Henry Coanda Airport)
one is assaulted even before reaching the gates with kitschy Dracula
figurines, fangs, caskets, and countless other bloody mementos. Here
myth meets marketing at its best, and with the power of the dollar
backing the fabrication of new and more eyecatching trinkets, history
seems to have thrown in the towel.

Yet no stereotype can do justice to Vlad Țepeș (Vlad the Impaler),
perhaps the most complicated figure in Romanian history. Like his father, Prince Vlad belonged the Order of the Dragon, a chivalric society
founded to defend Eastern Christendom from the Ottoman Empire;
hence the patronymic Dracula, Son of the Dragon. Vlad fought for and

came to symbolize Romanian independence. But Dracula also means Son of the Devil. Vlad tortured and killed his enemies by impaling them on spikes, drawing and quartering them, or nailing their fezzes to their skulls. His actions so appalled his subjects that, after death, his deeds became legend and remain notorious across the globe. All the more reason, then, to cash in on his bankable name. If Dracula is what the customers want, then Dracula is what they'll get—and Romania's tourist hotspots are often happy to oblige.

Can you blame them? The Dracula appropriated by American popular culture, the Eastern European bogey packaged in films, books, cartoons, and Halloween costumes, isn't actually Romanian, but it sure packs a big, entertaining punch, not to mention a hefty profit margin. The original character, created by the Irish author and theatrical agent, Abraham "Bram" Stoker, was modeled after Sir Henry Irving, the suave but cadaverous British actor who was Stoker's personal incubus. Béla Lugosi, who played the count on stage and screen, was a Hungarian actor whose success degenerated into typecasting and heroin addiction. Nevertheless, ethnicity aside, when I try to imagine Halloween in America without a single Dracula costume, I simply can't. The mere possibility of a Dracula moratorium boggles the mind. The media will never refrain from invoking his name and, by extension, his myth.

❦

Dracula—the man, the myth, the franchise—casts a shadow from which no one is able or willing to escape. A 2014 article on Smithsonian.com, simply titled "Dracula's Castle for Sale," shows the Dracula phenomenon's grip on the Western imagination. Relatively short, the article mostly concentrates on the current owners' intention to sell the castle for $80 million. However, the article also provides a short historical account of the castle and reveals a psychological blind spot about the Dracula myth, even in media outlets supposedly committed to accuracy and impartiality. After grabbing the reader's attention with the headline "Dracula's Castle," the article begins with the words "Bran

Castle," which is the castle's rightful and accurate name. The article then clarifies that the castle, in fact, has no real connection to Dracula, or more specifically to Vlad Ţepeş, the Romanian ruler who inspired Bram Stoker's fictional character.

While we might be tempted to give credit to the author for acknowledging history, we instead should question the intent and subsequent use of a headline that clearly balks at reality and skirts historical accuracy. Why would a prestigious cultural institution such as the Smithsonian insist on promoting and sustaining a myth that has long been debunked by historians and scholars? The answer might be as simple as "the story sells" and anyone therefore can exploit it to generate interest and revenue. To some extent, this partly explains why Romanians perpetrate Dracula-themed tourism, but simply to dismiss such hucksterism ignores its impact on our perception of culture and history.

As a function of what French sociologist Pierre Bourdieu calls *cultural capital* (something exchanged—sold or otherwise shared—for economic profit and cultural meaning), "Dracula" and all of its baggage become highly problematic, a vulgar symbol caped in its own self-perpetuating glamour. It is no exaggeration to say that Dracula is an internationally recognized brand name for evil. By extension, and according to common lore, evil then has definitive roots in Transylvania/Romania. Romania's cultural capital, therefore, becomes its cultural burden, a stereotype that easily fits Edward Said's description of the Oriental "other": violent, barbaric, exotic, and highly sexualized.

(⁶

Bucharest's Tourist Information Office, located in *Piaţa Universităţii* (University Square), tries to mitigate this damage by promoting actual Romanian history. One example might be found in *Lipscani*, Bucharest's medieval marketplace, which lies near the ruins of the old Princely Court, built by none other than Vlad the Impaler. Plaques and information signs on an iron fence invite tourists to stop and take pictures. Yet across the alley, barely a few feet away, lies an overpriced souvenir shop. It is impossible to reconcile history and commerce. They forever clash, and it's a fight in which the odds are woefully stacked against truth. After all, a few crumbling bricks and a stone column can hardly compete with the allure of Count Chocula cereal boxes or American TV.

Meanwhile, that peasant artisan who ekes out an existence in the foothills of Braşov can hardly be judged for wanting a piece of the action or for participating in a national publicity stunt. He takes a doll dressed in traditional folk costume, paints bloody fangs on its mouth, and calls it "Son of Dracula." In the face of market logic and economic necessity, culture be damned! But the Dracula chain flourishes because it extends beyond my homeland's borders. Romanians have exported and capitalized on their infamy across the Atlantic.

During the 2008 season of *America's Got Talent*, judge David Hasselhoff played the vampire card with Indiggo, a singing act of Romanian twin sisters. Born in Transylvania, Gabriela and Mihaela Modorcea billed themselves as "Dracula's Girls." When they performed an abysmal rendition of "New York, New York," Hasselhoff pantomimed fangs biting into his neck. He also mocked the twins in a campy Romanian accent, much to the delight of the crowd. To paraphrase Gary Oldman in *Bram Stoker's Dracula*, I have crossed oceans of time to join a minstrel show.

Romania, in the Western eye (and often its own) is more myth than reality, an imaginary place where fake *nosferatu* drain the blood of culture until it becomes kitsch. If vampires are not your cup of blood, try other horrors: the disintegration of Roma tradition, Dickensian orphanages and child trafficking, zombie communism, prostitution and mail-order brides. The Associated Press seldom reports on positive news coming out of Romania. Instead, it prefers to collect believe-it-or-not stories tailor-made for supermarket tabloids.

On June 15, 2008, Voineşti, a village in Dâmbovita County, southern Romania, reelected its recently dead major, Neculai Ivascu. The 6,200 residents refused to vote for Ivascu's rival, Gheorghe

Dobrescu, a candidate from the ruling National Liberal Party. "I know he died," one villager told reporters, "but I don't want change." This is Romania after all. Not even the dead rest in peace here. And, as long as there are buyers, neither will the myth.

On a Day between Seasons

Bucharest in June with a bucket when everything disappears through the false bottom. If I had to choose, this one is my favorite story from the library of nightmares. But they are all that good. Time as the devil of love. A madman who divides long enough until there are no remainders. The heartbroken widow walking home alone with a gold chain and an empty locket because she says she is trying to move on. On a day between seasons.

Bucharest in June with a bucket when the skies pour down as if someone threw open the deadbolt of night. I keep coming back to this one because it resembles the fragile infrastructure of longing. Like a carousel ride that always ends exactly where it began. A familiar pattern of doubt I no longer question. By the time the music stops it's so late that it's early and we turn ugly or beautiful according to each other's needs.

Bucharest in June with a bucket when I try to hold the water in my hands by making smaller buckets of skin. The rain comes down and falls through the false bottom, through the husk of myself like a second skin I've outgrown and which doesn't fool anyone. I watch the water pool around my ankles and I think to myself, I can't even remember what it's like not to drown.

Waiting Our Turn

We waited patiently in line. Generations had waited patiently before us and this was our only proper inheritance. Pardon me if I may say so, but we had gotten quite good at it, the way one does with any other acquired skill.

℀

At long last, which is a rough estimate, we were offered a proper hearing. It was decided that only a taxi would do for such an occasion. Not to mention the Sunday clothes, a fresh morning shave. We then took our time leaving in a hurry, flipping over the kitchen chair and slamming doors the way we assumed hurried people do when faced with important things and can't be bothered by details.

℀

Once there we pushed our way past much stone. The rain-battered columns, the grave mouth chiseled over the entrance. We couldn't help but admire how dignified he looked, coroner beautiful, dead by the whites of his eyes, nearly ravaged. A well-fed corpse we agreed.

℀

Once inside we were given instructions on proper etiquette, the importance of a lowered gaze. More waiting, but by then we were in fine form.

℀

When it was our turn to speak imagine the surprise—the envelope already bent with a red angry seal. Official business spins on very short wheels. We didn't have to say a single word.

℀

Outside, the buses appeared to be running more or less on schedule. The rain waiting patiently, too. And just our luck, only a very short line. Some would say an occasion to be grateful. Some always do.

Legends and Other Ordinary Things

On the wrong side of a broken door I cannot close, in the known uncertainty of twilight. I'm hunched over some square table digging at the yolk while the beggar sings a love song bouncing a small child on her bare knees. Tonight the two of them will follow me like ghosts over a one-way bridge. Dragging it all behind, the cup and the covenant, naked and shivering.

I tell you that nothing beautiful was built to last more than a lifetime despite our best intentions. That should be enough for most of us but very seldom is. And so we take it to the grave. We wrap the corpse and paint it for the birds to look at from the wire. Their voices drop like coins into a paper cup. Their voices drop like so many lost coins. And the old guitars keep playing variations of the blues in back alleys and dives, the dirtiest of cross town bars. You can't close the door on this one no matter how hard you try. It comes to you with gravel in its knees, naked and shivering, leaning on the short end of a stick.

I take the last train home and listen as it rattles on the outskirts of a dream. It chases the first burn of daylight like the good life colored in a storefront window. Only everything is interrupted. The last story to pick up its bags is filled with many ends and few beginnings. Then the long or short road waiting just beyond the station. And in the near distance ditches and the fields that draw the blood out of the cities just to make it look new again. A fine show if there ever was one. Green grass of summer swaying to the wind. The leaves naked, shivering.

Antonio

Bread and Circuses (Pt. 1)

WEST OF THE COLISEUM, now sponsored by shoe manufacturer Diego
Della Valle, who has donated $34 million to its restoration, sprawl
the imperial ruins of the Palatine Hill. Here on April 11, 2011, the
Special Superintendence for Rome's Archaeological Heritage opened
an exhibit devoted to the Emperor Nero. On display for the first time
were Nero's many architectural and cultural contributions, including a
recently excavated chamber believed to be the legendary *coenatio ro-
tunda*, a rotating dining hall with sweeping views onto the Alban Hills.

Any show about the notorious Nero was bound to attract visitors, but the superintendence had not anticipated its greatest turnout
in a decade. Movie stars, fat cats, and politicians mobbed the exhibit,
including Prime Minister Silvio Berlusconi, accompanied by a bevy of
sequined bimbos. The bright lights revealed the flaws in his face lift,
but the prime minister kept smiling at the cameras.

"Well, he's good box office," observes Roberto Gervaso, the bald
and hawk-eyed seventy-seven-year-old author of the 1978 biographical
novel *Nerone*. Did Gervaso mean Nero or Berlusconi? The old man
laughed at the reporter's question. "Nero, of course! They've made lots
of films about Nero, but they couldn't resist making a caricature of him.
There's no need to do that—he was a caricature himself."

Nero Claudius Caesar Augustus Germanicus, the last of the Ju-
lian-Claudian dynasty, was Rome's greatest showman. Only seventeen
when he became emperor, he remained a narcissist and an exhibition-
ist. He drove chariots, strummed the lyre, and recited poetry. If he
had been alive today, he would have entered talent contests, haunted
karaoke bars, or posted YouTube clips. Instead, he hijacked Rome's
entertainment complexes, such as the Circus Maximus, which seated
between 150,000 and 180,000 spectators, and inflicted his hamming

on the Senate and people. Nero turned Homer into air guitar, danced classical Greek ballet (despite spindly legs and a pot belly), and played gods and heroes and even heroines and goddesses in campy adaptations of Aeschylus and Sophocles.

"*While he performed,*" Suetonius reports, "*no one was allowed to leave the theatre even for the most urgent reasons. And so it is said that some women gave birth to children there, while many who were worn out with listening and applauding, secretly leaped from the wall, since the gates at the entrance were closed, or feigned death and were carried out as if for burial.*"

Nero dreaded that he was making a fool of himself. To preempt ridicule, he turned his enemies and subjects into laughingstocks. He compelled four hundred senators and six hundred knights to fight in the arena. He ordered charioteers to race with donkeys and camels. He forced acrobats to perform daredevil parodies of Greek myth. An unlucky Icarus fell too close to the imperial couch and spattered the emperor with blood. He cast a Cretan ballerina as Pasiphaë, made her squeeze into a wooden heifer, and had her mounted by a bull. Christians, of course, he dressed as scarecrows and set on fire.

The plebs did not know how to react to these spectacles, so Nero created claques. He selected five thousand hunky youths, easily recognizable by their bushy hair and spangled gowns, and divided them into three groups. The Bees made a loud humming sound. The Roof Tiles clapped with their hollowed hands; the Bricks, flat-handed. Whenever the crowds were confused by the sight of naked pregnant women fighting like gladiators, the claque cued them to laugh and applaud. No dead air in Nero's arena. He was a terrible emperor but a wonderful program director.

Nero never owned a television network. Nevertheless, he awarded himself an Emmy the size of the Statue of Liberty. He erected a one hundred foot bronze colossus of himself in the vestibule of the Domus Aurea or Golden House. Supposedly, the Emperor had set fire to Rome to make room for this vast complex, spanning the north side of the Palatine, across the Velian ridge to the Esquiline Hill. Standing outside the main entrance at the end of the Appian Way in a large atrium of porticoes, the statue held a rudder on a globe, symbolizing Nero's power over land and sea.

Such extravagance antagonized the Senate and alienated the provinces. When the armies rebelled in Gaul and Hispania and marched on Rome, the carnival was over. Before being dispatched by his secretary, the emperor cried, "*Qualis artifex pereo!*" What an artist dies in me! The Senate declared Nero anathema and erased his name from monuments, but the populace mourned him. He had provided so much free entertainment.

Nero's more prudent successors capitalized on this nostalgia. Vespasian added a sun-ray crown to his statue and renamed it Colossus Solis, after the Roman sun god Sol. Hadrian later moved the landmark to make room for the Temple of Venus and Roma. Two dozen elephants hauled the colossus northwest from the Domus Aurea to the Flavian Amphitheater, renamed the Coliseum in its honor.

Two thousand years later, at the Archeological Heritage's mixer on the Palatine, modern Romans pondered Nero's legacy. Count Andrea Carandini, professor of archeology at Sapienza University, warmed to the subject. Nero turned myth into politics, politics into spectacle. The Roman games became bloody and mindless mass entertainment: a distraction from drudgery and oppression, a safety valve for frustration and resentment. They provided the only direct communion between rulers and the masses, who were no longer free citizens but a captive audience. "This is television!" Carandini exclaimed. "Silvio Berlusconi did exactly the same thing, using the media to connect with the plebs."

Walter Vetroni, Rome's former mayor, who once served as Italy's minister of culture, rejected the comparison. Whatever his faults, Nero at least had appreciated archeology. "Berlusconi, in contrast, has no interest in archeology," Vetroni said. "The word is simply not in his head."

Andrei

Parallel Vista

Sometimes all you need to do is climb higher to see how it all falls back into the sea. The armless statues naked from the waist, the columns jittery and peeling like dead skin. Sea-blue houses on the Greek coast, the beach growing at your feet while under canopies of grass we sip drinks with matching straws. The easy chairs in the sun are lined up like dominoes and the anchored boats are at half-mast. The sea endless in its calm.

🌓

In the next town over the donkeys are being prepared for the next climb. Carrots and all. A jagged cliff of broken windmills waits for the onslaught of photographs, the smiling Don Quixotes not too far from the real thing. The locals shut their mouths because they know hot air rises and falls with each phase of the moon.

🌓

When the chill of night descends from the hills it empties the sand, which we didn't talk about enough these days. The sand at our feet. And now in the dark of a hotel window, the shutters pushed open as far as they could go, it becomes hard to tell where it begins and where it ends. Miles away and beyond us. Where they have other things to worry about, if they wonder at all.

Exit Strategy

History had thrown down its gauntlet. It unraveled at the poorly knotted seam, became a charlatan's playground, scattered with the day's unfinished business.

⟢

I was scared to be alone, to be left alone in this dread apartment with its single myopic window. I walked out in the suffocating heat, thin lights of this backwater navigated by stars, insomniac children, and the dogs that nip at their heels.

⟢

The only model citizens were statues of copper and marble, companions walking with me into some primitive doctrine—the wind hurling itself against the gray buildings, nameless uncelebrated martyrs, grown out of nothing, nothing torn against nothing, as the town slept under a star-dirty sky and pictures of the zodiac were being doctored for the morning news.

⟢

Wax was on everyone's lips. Smoke of the bloodied alphabet overflowed ashtrays. Cheap crystal shone in the neon climate. A few cafes open late while the lone sullen waitress tinkered with the glass rearranging sugar. Red velvet chairs questioning her every move, a theater of the perfectly absurd . . .

⟢

Swollen porcelain eye, breath asleep in its own pallid skin, wing and bone, black water white fountain, ribbon that could never be undone, forgotten gardens and rust, overgrown ivy, tendrils and roots, litter climbing the alleys, smell of alcohol and rye, sidewalk music and habitual sex, the common cure in apothecary bottles, barricades and cocktails, new shoe leather and oil . . .

❦

But now all of it is left for dead. Worse than that. Forgotten. That's how it felt. Buried breathing. Last gasp, dearth of air. Stem of life on someone else's terms, obedient, patient, stuck inside a flowerpot and dirt.

❦

And all of us headed home in cramped cars and subways, riding the cry and groan of the rail. Cantata of our daily grief begun inside the rotting teeth of twilight. Songs and declarations soaked in rose petal perfume, store-counter women humming along daydreaming through the dark days and the not so dark. I send along my sleep-deprived dreaming, my discreet love and the tender grammar of a smile I can bear to part with for your sake . . .

❦

For your sake and my own. For the selfish man that is a gift and a burden. The streets are abused with our pounding, these two fists bleeding a silent cry beating the arid breast of this, our hallowed ground. I alone in the madhouse, I and the few other mad ones, I and all of us mad, I of the universe, I suffocating, I trying to make out the impure outline of it, I alone before the I, something not yet made into a witness.

The Future Is Best Eaten with a Wooden Spoon

Your old city is rotting, it smells, it is drowning in spring. Unending rains are pummeling the home where you became a child. On the open balcony the clothes are hung with twine.

In a dream a cross sleeps broken in pieces. Name beside name wiped clean of its life. Only the wax pours always gentle and timid, yellow on your fingers—

and with dust and wind it washes its hands, and with breath and tongues it grows into its wooden memories. Thick as a palm raised to the sky. Light as a fist of fog.

What's missing from so much nothingness fulfilled? Only sweet departure, and from time to time a new arrival.

But lately you've misplaced yourself—between empty trolleys, uninhabited streets, in the city old and blind, scratching at its hide.

Do you know yourself inside the many shop windows? In the mark of fresh paint, fingers firm, stuck to the cemetery fence?

It's here that you've fallen, here that you went head over heels. Here the streets lie drawn and quartered, splayed like a tattered circle.

In another dream, this along the alley of roses, yesterday's water smiles back at you. Lovers love as only they know, tear the petals of eternal flowers.

And if such madness were not enough, the stones are bent over—some praying on their knees, some hiding a mischievous grin. But you know, and they know, and much goes unsaid.

Antonio

Bread and Circuses (Pt. 2)

DURING HIS SATURNALIAN RULE, the longest since Benito Mussolini, Italians often asked: "Which Roman emperor does Silvio Berlusconi most resemble?" Classicists thumbed through their Tacitus and Suetonius. Like Otho, Berlusconi was vain. To compensate for his pug face and short stature, he resorted to hair plugs, tanning salons, plastic surgery, and orthopedic shoes. Like Tiberius, he preyed on minors. At the bunga-bunga parties in his Sardinian villa, he leered as underaged escorts dressed as meter maids and nuns stripped and danced. Like Nero, he sang off key and fiddled while Rome burned. A gold-plated sun god, he eclipsed his country's glory and turned politics into a circus.

Others, however, compared the Italian prime minister to Trimalchio, the crass and exhibitionistic millionaire in Gaius Petronius Arbiter's *Satyricon*. "The old political parties," said Alexander Stille, author of *The Sack of Rome; How a Beautiful European Country with a Fabled History and a Storied Culture Was Taken Over by a Man Named Silvio Berlusconi* (2006), "the Christian Democratic Party and the Communist Party, represented broad ideologies and their leaders were comparatively unimportant. Berlusconi, already a celebrity, offered himself: no real ideology other than his own personal wealth."

A former vacuum cleaner salesman and cruise ship crooner, Silvio Berlusconi was Italy's richest man: a media tycoon worth seven billion dollars, who also owned AC Milan, the country's most popular soccer team. Berlusconi was a cheerleader and a showman. A raunchier Italian version of Ronald Reagan, he believed in the miracle of free markets and exuded confidence and optimism. "A good salesman," he bragged, "always carries the sun in his pocket." Using the most advanced marketing, polling, and advertising techniques, Berlusconi created a new political party, Forza Italia (after the football cheer "Go,

Italy!"). He promised to revive Italy's entrepreneurial spirit, deregulate its industry, shrink its government, and usher in a new age of prosperity. "Your program," he told Confindustria, Italy's most powerful business consortium, "is my program." But the only program he cared about was his own.

Berlusconi entered politics to protect his communications empire from regulators. Mediaset, Italy's largest broadcasting company, monopolized commercial television. Mondadori, Italy's most important publishing house, printed most of its trade books and magazines. *Il Giornale*, owned by Berlusconi's brother Paolo, was the country's most influential center-right newspaper. Publitalia, the family advertising agency, produced nearly all the spots on Mediaset's television channels. Berlusconi was thus in the happy position of being able to pay himself to advertise his own products on his own networks.

Berlusconi's most important product, of course, was his image. After becoming prime minister, he maintained control of Mediaset but also hijacked Radiotelevisione Italiana (RAI), the national public broadcasting company. This takeover, however, was merely the coup de grace. Berlusconi already had syphoned most of RAI's viewers, who were more interested in watching Emanuele Filiberto di Savoia compete on *Dancing with the Stars* than a dramatic series on his great-great-grandfather Victor Emanuel II.

Desperate to compete with Mediaset, Italy's three state channels had swapped documentaries, opera telecasts, and lectures on art, history, and literature for a merry-go-round of game shows, talk shows, phone-ins, and soft porn. Berlusconi merely took the next logical step. He fired the RAI's directors and replaced them with hand-picked flunkies and cronies. The prime minister not only had the power to make the news. He also could command public and commercial networks to report it as prominently and favorably as possible.

Berlusconi's control of the media perverted Italian politics. Serious and responsible newspapers, which had refused to concede to popular taste, were ignored. Outspoken journalists were bullied and silenced. During a visit to Bulgaria, Berlusconi denounced three journalists who had either mocked him or allowed someone to mock him on TV: the trio were fired and effectively banned from working in television. The sledgehammer irony was pure *opera buffa*. Berlusconi used his own formidable mass media apparatus to accuse the mass media of persecuting him. Freedom House, a political watchdog group, downgraded Italy's press status from "free" to "partly free." Italy fell to seventy-third in the world's rankings, below Ghana, Chile, Mali, and Namibia.

With freedom of speech curtailed, Umberto Eco noted, "artists [were] the only people to inspire argument and debate, obviously without being able to suggest solutions." Roberto Benigni, the donkey-faced comedian, shocked and delighted the audience at the San Remo Festival. "Please, Berlusconi," he pleaded, "please do something that, when we go to bed at night, will make us proud to be Italians." Maestro Riccardo Muti interrupted a performance of Verdi's *Nabucco* to mourn the state of the country. Moved, the audience joined the conductor and the La Scala cast in the Chorus of the Hebrew Slaves, the great Risorgimento hymn. Thinking of their own Babylonian exile, they wept and sang: "*O mia patria, sì bella e perduta! O membranza sì cara e fatal!*" O my country, so beautiful and lost. O memory, so dear and so fatal.

Berlusconi was deaf to such appeals. When he surveyed Italy's cultural heritage, its forty-four UNESCO World Heritage sites, its five thousand museums and sixty thousand archeological digs, a natural resource richer than Middle Eastern oil, he saw only a business opportunity. Following the advice of University of Chicago consultants, the prime minister reduced the national budget for historic preservation to less than 0.2 percent, sold off government-owned Etruscan villas, medieval monasteries, and Baroque palazzos, and surrendered the usage rights to corporate sponsors.

What was the result of this privatization? The Temple of Demeter at Agrigento deteriorated, and the House of the Gladiators at Pompeii collapsed, perhaps irreparably. In Rome, the roof of Nero's Golden House crumbled, and a section of the Coliseum fell to the ground. Despite protests, the draconian cuts continued. "I don't know what all the fuss is about," said Berlusconi's economics minister Giulio Tremonti.

"After all, you can't eat culture."

Few Italians cared. As the Slovenian philosopher Slavoj Žižek observes, Berlusconi's crass Philistinism, his complete indifference to Italian history and utter contempt for Italian art, actually convinced voters to "identify with him as embodying the mythic image of the average Italian: I am one of you, a little bit corrupt, in trouble with the law, in trouble with my wife because I'm attracted to other women. Even his grandiose enactment of the role of the noble politician, *il cavaliere*, [was] more like an operatic poor man's dream of greatness."

Consequently, the public always forgave Berlusconi's gaffes. When he praised U.S. President Barack Obama's "youthful suntan," compared the plight of the tent-sheltered survivors of the L'Aquila earthquake to "a weekend of camping," or called German Chancellor Angela Merkel "an unfuckable lard-ass," he winked and invited voters to laugh at feminists, communists, and eggheads. "Leftists," he said, "have no sense of humor."

But behind the clownish mask Berlusconi governed with ruthless efficiency. He considered himself a *uomo forte*, a classic political strong man, and praised Mussolini. Il Duce, Berlusconi insisted, had not "murdered anyone." On the contrary, his dictatorship had been "benign." He had punished his opponents not by jailing them but by sending them "on holiday" to islands in the Mediterranean. These comments endeared him to the National Alliance, Italy's old neofascist party (the MSI) with a new name, which kept Berlusconi in power. When Alessandra Mussolini, the movie star turned politician, autographed pictures of her grandfather during a parliamentary debate, the prime minister shrugged and flashed a Cheshire grin. People have a right to dispose of their family memorabilia as they see fit.

Berlusconi was no joke. For Žižek, he embodies the moral bankruptcy of democratic capitalism, the growing danger of demagogic populism, and the domestication of totalitarianism. Like his friend, Russian President Vladmir Putin, Berlusconi ultimately represents "the human face of barbarism," tyranny as a form of self-parodying comedy. As long as people see through the joke, they will settle for the ironic consolations of entertainment rather than risk the struggles of freedom. Deprivation, however, can jolt even the most passive couch potatoes into revolt.

When Italy's debt crisis required austerity measures, Berlusconi fell. He barely survived a no-confidence vote in the Senate, but further defections cost him a majority. A guard quoted a popular proverb: "A tenor is applauded until he is booed off stage." As the disgraced prime minister arrived at the Quirinal Palace, a hostile crowd gathered. They carried banners, shouted insults, and flung coins at his limo. Wearing scarlet-mantled togas and masks of Berlusconi as a chapleted Nero, protesters marched down Via del Corso chanting "Resign, resign!"

After Berlusconi conceded to President George Napolitano, jeers and whistles followed the retreating convoy. "*Buffone!*" people shouted. "*Mafioso!*" An orchestra played the "Hallelujah Chorus" from Handel's *Messiah* and the *Dies Irae* from Mozart's *Requiem*. People sang and danced in the streets. Cars and mopeds in downtown Rome waved Italian flags and honked their horns in celebration.

Two years later, Silvio Berlusconi finally was convicted of tax fraud. Prosecutors had proved that Mediaset, his broadcasting company, had overpaid for film rights to reduce its tax liability. Berlusconi was sentenced to four years in prison but a general amnesty reduced it to one year. "If only he'd been convicted of handing out free focaccia, too!" crowed Natalie Hayne, a reporter for *The Independent*. "We could have had the first case of bread and circuses since the satirist Juvenal coined the phrase."

VI

Eternal Recurrences

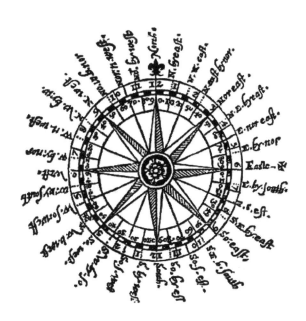

Andrei

A Blueprint for Memory (Redux)

LET US RETURN to that tortured artist trying to draw a house in the first chapter only to have each portion erased as soon as he completed it. But since history is a palimpsest, always prone to erasure, let's make life a little more difficult for him. Let's make him into an artist who wants to draw his childhood home, but who no longer remembers what the house actually looked like. Mind you, he has a clear Platonic *idea* about this house. It represents every conceivable Old World homecoming from Odysseus to Leopold Bloom. He's just a little fuzzy about the homey details. Was the house made of stucco or brick? Was it shingled with tiles or thatched with straw?

So he asks for help. A grandmother tells him a story about how swallows used to nest in the eaves, and now he seems to remember the eaves. His father chuckles when he recalls the young artist lifting himself up to look out the window. Now the house has a window that looks like what it might have looked back then. Someone also brings out a dusty box with old photographs and in some of them there is a corner of the house, a wall, a roof, maybe a door. The artist now goes back and revises. He listens, he remembers, he revises. He stumbles across an object, an image, some relic, and he again revises. He works at this house for a lifetime, so long that eventually all who remember are no longer around.

But he's insistent; he wants to finish what he's started. Nathan Oliveira said, "*All art is a series of recoveries from the first line. The hardest thing to do is to put down the first line. But you must.*" And so what is missing our artist invents; he takes his best guess and turns it into a line on paper, solid enough that it feels right, that it feels just as he would have remembered it. When the house is finally complete, when it resembles the collective memory of all that he's cobbled together, who's left to say that it wasn't so? He is the architect of that house, of its memory, and he is its sole caretaker, the authority on how it was, how it is, and how it will be. In the end, what he's created is a version of *house*, a version of the past, as real to him as any other.

The house that our artist has created could very well be considered a product of postmemory, a term coined by Marianne Hirsch, the William Peterfield Trent Professor of English and Comparative Literature at Columbia University. On her website, www.postmemory.net, the Romanian-born Hirsch describes postmemory as

> the relationship that the "generation after" bears to the personal, collective, and cultural trauma of those who came before to experiences they "remember" only by means of the stories, images, and behaviors among which they grew up. But these experiences were transmitted to them so deeply and affectively as to seem to constitute memories in their own right. Postmemory's connection to the past is thus actually mediated not by recall but by imaginative investment, projection, and creation. To grow up with overwhelming inherited memories, to be dominated by narratives that preceded one's birth or one's consciousness, is to risk having one's own life stories displaced, even evacuated, by our ancestors. It is to be shaped, however indirectly, by traumatic fragments of events that still defy narrative reconstruction and exceed comprehension. These events happened in the past, but their effects continue into the present.

The website includes an abstract for a keynote address (*Small Acts of Repair: The Unclaimed Legacy of Transnistria*) that Hirsch delivered with Leo Spitzer (Dartmouth College). The focus here is on art and its role in remembrance:

> Since postmemory is unable to draw on precise recollections, great importance is given to imagination and creation. Art has a major part to play in this process, since in some cases it is only through the works created by survivors that subsequent generations can access the traumatic event. Art also constitutes an ideal means

for later generations to attempt to imagine an unknown past and discover its implications in their lives.

Key words in the language of Hirsch's writings seem to be projection, creation, imagine, and repair. We can see how all of those terms played an important role in our artist's rendering of his house. As many who engage in actions of postmemory, he salvaged the memory of that house, preserved it, and likely will pass it on.

But at what cost? Hirsch claims that postmemory has the potential to replace one's own memories and sense of reality with that of those who actually experienced the past. When this occurs, one risks becoming a medium for a bunch of unreliable ghosts. Yet there might not be a choice in the matter—we all suffer the past in one way or another. We stand on the shoulders of giants but we also haul them on our backs willingly or not.

But it is not mere remembrance that keeps our artist up at night—it is the creative act itself that troubles him much more. He not only imagined, he (re)imagined. He not only created, he re(created). He did not only repair the house, he redesigned it from the ground up.

And as any good artist does, he revises—obsessively—going over what he's already created because he seeks perfection. Like a modern-day Matisse, he creates different versions of his house to see which one looks the best. They're lined up all over his studio. You can pick and choose the one that suits your needs. When you're bored with that one, simply trade it in for a newer version.

Insert Inspirational Slogan Here

We stand before a three-piece mirror that would break us apart and make us whole again; make us in turn the loneliest of men. We know what it means despite a pouring dark that soaks us to the bone.

Who's got us up his sleeve tonight? Someone always does. We are the spades or hearts in a pity hand, just enough for a couch on credit. As is. Just enough to take your darling out for a good time and give it all over to fate.

And when you finally get used to it they will come around and mess with the color scheme. New T-shirts with old Soviet propaganda for another imitation poster life. The art of hammer and sickle peddled at a New York market stall. Where the hustler puts a tear in the otherwise stern eye and looks at you with that fresh twist of nostalgia—the oldest trick in the book.

Isn't it always like that when some years have passed? You watch an old man dying on a rainy afternoon as he looks out through the memory of an open window. The smell of the apple orchard. That village taste behind the curtain of a million drops lined up like orphans with their eyes against the soft horizon of a new age.

What everyone seems to remember from this picture are the apples. Iconic sheen of green. That at the end, before the credits roll too fast over his grave, the old man appears happy. Something to talk on the way home.

Talking Old Country Blues

Valley where the flowers grow long for crown and laurel.

Place where the open eye takes fill of its weeping blue.

Home where the gallows cry to be untied from their affliction.

Your bones recall a weekend rendezvous rouged in lilac and clover. But each season brings an end to how color feels beneath skin. Furrow and the solid line sweeps to the left and right of your owned vision; unspools into the living stone that grinds away at a common wheel, stubborn through murkiest ditch. And no break or solace whatsoever in the clouds that congregate like moss, below the drag and pull of a true north, sure as wind claiming the water's edge.

That dreamland is now well into overtime hours and the end is at the matchmaker's whim. From slum to mountainside all it took to make a man believe and set him on his twisted course is a parting of sky. Something above the plunge of moral highroads—released from a child's hand, floating upward, grieving with each gust, meeting the white snow of silence where it shrivels, takes time to fall back to the soft folds of history.

And when you decide to go looking for it again, lowering the rope into some kind of primitive sleep, what will you find along the riverbed of your palm? Green blood and borders. Out of reach horizon. Arguments that won't be put on hold for dinner or the rain of cold and dreary afternoons. Neither for the glare of trumpets.

It Could Have Been a Dream

I had no choice but to look for them where the fish turned back. Their horses were tethered to trees and their bones had begun to show. Some were on one bank and some languished stranded on the opposite shore. The sound of the sea was not far off, just as we had learned in grade school.

What appeared to be distance was only the rickety architecture of the mind. Great ships were scattered like landmarks on some old country road. I heard a few of the dying give thanks that we made it here in the first place. Christ, I thought, we've forgotten how to get wet anymore; they set us free and we've forgotten—our feet made of the lead bullets of youth that fall and pierce the ground before the wind comes along in its fullness and does away with the rest. Nothing left to do but build a fire and wait for the first light.

Was the rest of it even real—the backyard nights when we made our own fires, sat slumping in metal chairs dangling cigarettes from our mouths? The bottles we passed back and forth between us that never seemed to go empty? Now we search blindly for the trap door marked with an exit sign. On the other side the old graybeards hovering and pointing at what seems to be a footprint. Some new dream we might follow.

Antonio

Nietzsche in Turin (Pt. 1)

TURIN IS AN ENIGMA. The capital of Italy's Piedmont region and the home of Fiat, Lavazza, and Olivetti, this northern metropolis is a model of efficiency and rationality. Because Guarino Guarini, priest, mathematician, and master architect, had laid out its center with such geometric precision, Turin—unlike most other Italian cities—could embrace modernization in the nineteenth and early twentieth centuries. The Ospedale Cottolengo, the city's clinic for the poor since 1832, combines in its design Baroque Catholicism and the Industrial Revolution. The Porta Nuova Train Station, opened in 1861, contains a large saloon, decorated with columns, stucco work and frescoes depicting the crests of 135 Italian cities and showing their exact distance in kilometers from Turin. The Lingotto Building, the old car factory on Via Nizza, now a concert hall, convention center, and hotel, is a triumph of town planning.

But for all its sunny logic and bustling optimism, Turin exudes an air of mystery and melancholy. Some blame the fog that can descend without warning and obliterate the Italian Alps. Poor visibility caused Turin's worst disaster. On May 4, 1949, an Alitalia airliner carrying the city's soccer team crashed into a hill and nearly destroyed the Basilica of Superga. Others, however, claim that Turin is haunted by the death of Christ. His ghostly image is stenciled on the famous shroud preserved in the Sacra Sindone Chapel, located outside the Cathedral of St. John the Baptist and connected to the Royal Palace.

Whatever the reason, Cesare Pavese rightly called Turin "a city of dreams." Its vast squares and endless arcades, immortalized in the paintings of Giorgio de Chirico, alienate and confuse. Anxiety fills its broad avenues, impervious to pedestrian and motor traffic. The Mole Antonelliana, the city's most prominent landmark, towers like a ziggurat on Via Montebello. Turiners compare it to the Tower of Babel, but it is a confusion of images, not sounds. Designed as a synagogue, this Moorish revival building now houses the National Museum of Cinema.

Turin's magic can be fatal. Torquato Tasso, Jean Jacques Rousseau, and J. A. Symonds suffered nervous breakdowns here. Primo Levi, a native son, committed suicide. But none succumbed more to Turin's spell than Friedrich Nietzsche, who lived for ten months in a boarding house beside the city post office on Piazza Carlo Alberto. During this stay, perhaps the happiest period in his life, the German philosopher experienced a final epiphany before going mad.

☾

Nietzsche arrived in April 1888. For the previous nine years, ever since resigning his position as professor of philology at Basel University, he had wandered all over Europe, forever seeking health and peace of mind to write, but he fell passionately in love with Turin. It was the most unlikely of romances. Nietzsche hated bourgeois mercantilism but was drawn to the Galleria dell'Industria Subalpina, a glass-roofed arcade of shops and offices, where he ate spumoni at the Caffé Romano and listened to the orchestra play Rossini. He detested Prussian militarism but admired the city's monuments to its dead heroes. The equestrian statue of Charles Albert of Sardinia, with its cocked hat and drawn saber, dominated the square in front of Palazzo Carmignano. The statue of Ferdinand of Genoa, even more dramatic, showed the Savoy prince urging his men forward even though his mortally wounded horse has fallen to its knees.

Such chauvinism should have aggravated Nietzsche's dyspepsia, but Piedmontese cuisine had improved his digestion. He devoured everything on the Hotel Nazionale's menu: *bros, risotto, ossobuco*, broccoli with garlic and anchovies, *torta alla Monferrina*, all washed down with Carpano vermouth. These meals fortified him for long and vigorous walks along the Po. His mind whirled with a new project, an intellectual autobiography called *Ecce Homo*, but the rushing water often reminded him of an old obsession: the riddle of time. We can never step in the same river twice, Heraclitus said, but Nietzsche believed that we could. A year earlier, in the first edition of *The Gay Science*, he had proposed the concept of Eternal Recurrence.

Nietzsche first conceived this idea in August 1881, while hiking through the woods beside Lake Silvaplana in the Swiss Grisons. Standing on the shore and observing the scudding clouds and the rippling water, he experienced a revelation. Time, he realized, did not fly in a straight line like an arrow. It undulated like water. This insight was reinforced the following April, during a three-week vacation in Sicily. Like Empedocles before him, Nietzsche was fascinated by the surf near Taormina. Wave after wave pounded against the base of the cliffs. Each surged greedily into every nook and cranny of the rock face, as if sluicing for gold, and then flowed back, a bit more slowly but still frothing with emotion. Was it disappointed or had it found what it sought? But already another wave was approaching, more greedily and savagely than the first, and it too crested, crashed, and churned with a lust to dig up treasures.

"Thus live waves," Nietzsche concluded. "Thus live we who will." If life is an endlessly recurring tide, then the cosmos has no purpose. If it has no purpose, it has no creator, no beginning or end. Time, therefore, is infinite. But because physical phenomena are finite, events must repeat themselves, exactly and forever.

Fin de siècle physicists would have objected. Even Henri Poincaré's recurrence theorem, which resembles your hypothesis, Dr. Nietzsche, proposes that certain energy systems will, after a sufficiently long time, return to a state very close to but not identical to their initial state. Besides, granted that space is finite and time infinite, it is still possible to set a small number of objects in motion so that they never repeat their initial position (or any other), *ad infinitum*. Nietzsche would have smiled. "Gentlemen," he would have said, "this is philosophy, not science," and would have performed the following thought experiment.

Suppose an angel or demon appeared to you and said: "This life as you now live it and have lived it, you will have to live once more and innumerable times more; and there will be nothing new in it, but every pain and every joy and every thought and sigh and everything unutterably small or great in your life will have to return to you, all in the same succession and sequence." Would this annunciation crush you, gentlemen, *or* lead you to transform your lives? Would you sentence yourselves to an eternity of drudgery and boredom and disappointment, to stuffy mornings in the lab, cold borscht for lunch, and licit intercourse in the evening, or would you choose to lead a life of beauty, excitement, and vitality?

Science is the new faith of our age, and scientists its white-coated priests, but science will never restore our faith in life, gentlemen. Life is meant to be lived, not known. Whether we really get to live it over again eternally isn't the point. The point is to live it here and now.

Andrei

Always the Small Things

The ocean licked its blue brow clean of bounded sky and sand and red hair cleaving at the wind. We stood there face to face with twilight, made our palms make fists in our pockets to hold on to something. What was said before wouldn't fit here—sometimes colors match out of coincidence and we make more of it than it really is. And sometimes it's those small things—no, always the small things—the waning light, brittle as a word caught in the mouth, and the lightest touch that could make it all topple over—knees down among the rushes, tall blades pushing through the grains, not even knowing what it is we've lost.

On the Outside Looking In

They were supposed to wait for me. Behind a red door smoking their usual cigarettes, drinking their wine. In each lap a pair of locked hands that had forgotten how to pray. Tall mirrors dusty from years of being left alone with their work.

𝅖

It might have been raining outside or it might have been a pleasant dusk—the blind windows bolted against trembling light. The clock's evenness pointing with urgency at what has yet to be finished. In the streets everyone walking halfway to somewhere. The good dog on an open porch hopes that it hasn't been forgotten. Wags his tail dreaming of a pat on the head.

𝅖

Was I gone so long that the exchange of false pity could no longer be postponed? It was only a promise, something children say, but they were supposed to wait for me.

𝅖

A cat passes by, the dog is sleeping, it keeps passing by. She reminds me of someone who must have loved and moved on without making a sound.

𝅖

Someone's brought out the drinks. They are dealing cards now. Everything I remember is being shuffled and cut, shuffled and cut again with a delicate gesture. I don't know how but I am on one of those cards. The one now with its face down, awaiting its turn.

How It Was and How It Should Be
(When Death Happens at a Distance)

—for my grandfather

They found him in the turned fields of May. One arm outstretched for a pillow, the knees gathered in, bony and thin. He'd laid down after a day's labor, after all the labors of his life. There was a breeze coming in off the lake and the soft bellows of cattle, the valley stretching on like canvas, ready for color. His child-soft hair lifted and turned like a leaf caught in a current, a feather in time.

☙

Or maybe he lay twisted in the mud of February with the rags of morning soaked down to the skin. The plum trees standing as naked arbiters of inauspicious moments. Any sound that morning would have carried for miles through the frozen air. There was instead the silence of the powerless, of those who know. And the dog that kept circling the yard like a dumb beast.

☙

When they got there he was with a clear glass in hand. Another one down on the table, dark from the wine. His ashtray smile filled the room, the cigarettes unfinished in their box. The old television played the game in black and white; the bed was made. Everything folded. Nearby some tools and greasy engine parts still waiting to be put together. Tomorrow. The neighbors would be coming down the road any minute with dishes and pans, a bottle of something strong.

Antonio

Nietzsche in Turin (Pt. 2)

"Have you ever said Yes to a single joy?" Zarathustra asks his disciples. "O my friends, then you have said Yes, too, to all woe. All things are entangled, ensnared, enamored; if ever you wanted one thing twice, if ever you said, 'You please me, happiness! Abide, moment!' then you wanted all back. All anew, all eternally, all entangled, ensnared, enamored—oh then you loved the world. Eternal Ones, love it eternally and evermore; and to woe, too, you say: 'Go, but return!'"

Nietzsche, who turned forty-four on October 15, 1888, had recurring fears that he would die young like his father. According to the family physician, the thirty-five-year-old Lutheran pastor had succumbed to *Gehirnerweichung* (literally "softening of the brain"), a vague medical term that can mean anything from encephalitis to apoplexy; but autopsy records suggest that he actually died of a brain tumor. Nietzsche, prone to migraines since childhood, always dreaded the possibility that his father's condition was hereditary. Biographers, however, suspect that Nietzsche had contacted syphilis in 1865 at a Cologne brothel, his first and possibly last sexual encounter.

German Romantics, who glamorized consumption and opium addiction, considered syphilis a sacred disease. Adrian Leverkühn, the hero of Thomas Mann's *Dr. Faustus*, deliberately infects himself to stimulate his genius. The spirochetes attacking the brain resemble sperm, impregnating the mind with divine thoughts. Like a brood of ouroboroi, these microscopic snakes devour their own tails, linking birth and death, and transform their victim, however briefly, into a god. The actual pathology is less poetic. The bacteria dissolve the meninges, the spongy membrane protecting the central nervous system, corkscrew into the cerebral cortex, and devour the cerebrum and cerebellum. The neurological damage causes headaches, tics, confusion, spasms, and hallucinations. Bouts of depression alternate with bursts of manic energy. As the brain loses mass, the mind effervesces in psychosis. This stage is followed by dementia, paralysis, and death.

Nietzsche sensed impending disintegration. Among his last papers was an aborted parable of Dionysus Zagreus, dismembered by the titans, restored by the gods, strolling along the banks of the Po. Beginning in November, he exhibited symptoms. His lips twisted into a grimace, noticeable even beneath his walrus moustache. His beautiful handwriting, intricate as a Bach fugue, became illegible. He cried whenever he heard music, even the frothiest Offenbach overture. Because his bedroom window faced the rear of Palazzo Carignano, he began to suspect that he was a secret member of the House of Savoy and asked to be addressed as royalty. An imaginary terrier accompanied him on his walks, a tin drinking cup clenched in its teeth.

On January 3, 1889, Nietzsche fainted while rescuing a draft horse on Piazza Carlo Alberto. The nag had collapsed from exhaustion, and the carter was whipping the beast till it bled. Bystanders were too horrified to react, but Nietzsche howled, threw his arms around the horse's neck, and—sobbing wildly—shielded it from further blows. Perhaps Nietzsche wanted life to imitate art. He had read *Crime and Punishment* and was struck by the passage in which Raskolnikov, Dostoevsky's would-be Superman, dreams of embracing a flogged horse. Nietzsche had had a similar dream the previous May. Perhaps he was acting out a fantasy. Ferdinand of Savoy had embraced his fallen horse before ordering a charge at the Battle of Novara, a gesture immortalized in Alfonso Balzico's equestrian statue in Piazza Solferino. Nietzsche often passed this monument on his walks. Perhaps, Milan Kundera speculates, the German philosopher was refuting Descartes, who claimed that animals have no souls because they lack reason—a last rejection of the dominance, the arrogance of the human mind over nature, of modern civilization's blind worship of progress. Whatever the explanation, Nietzsche's desperate act of compassion began his final descent into madness.

Summoned by the *carabinieri*, Davide Fino, Nietzsche's landlord, carried the philosopher back home. Nietzsche regained consciousness but began behaving oddly. He barked commands in German, claiming to be Kaiser Wilhelm. He ordered his room to be painted with frescoes so he could receive King Umberto and Queen Margherita. He accosted strangers in Piazza Carlo Alberto and announced the death of God. He locked himself in the parlor and improvised midnight rhapsodies on the piano. Signora Fino knelt by the keyhole and saw him cavorting in the nude. Neighbors called him a *cutu*, a mental case for the Cottolengo asylum. When he wrote letters about partitioning Europe, redecorating the Vatican, and executing anti-Semites, signed alternately Dionysus and the Crucified, relatives finally came to fetch him.

Before leaving, Nietzsche asked for one last favor. "Dear Signor Fino," he said, "may I have your *papalina*?" He wanted Fino's triangular, tasseled nightcap for the journey back to Basel. When he put it on, he resembled a mock pope at a Roman carnival.

𝄘

A decade after the German Antichrist's departure, the Shroud of Turin was exhibited for the first time. In May 1898, to celebrate the four hundredth anniversary of its cathedral, the city petitioned King Umberto to display and photograph the relic: a linen cloth with ketchup-colored bloodstains and the faint outline of a human body wrapped around a wooden dowel and stored in a silver chest in the Savoy Chapel. While Secondo Pia, the official photographer, was developing an image of the shroud, Christ's face practically jumped out of the negative. Exposition posters already had been printed, so it was impossible to include the image in the promotions, but the photograph ran the next month in all the major Italian papers. Postcards were sold in Catholic gift shops in Europe and America. *Ecce homo!*

Since then Christ's face has appeared in burned bacon fat at the bottom of a frying pan and in spilled fabric softener on a stained T-shirt, on a Pizza Hut billboard and on a breakfast burrito, now enshrined in Lake Arthur, New Mexico. If the Son of God cannot escape merchandising, what hope remains for us mere mortals who are human, all too human? Even Nietzsche, the man who rejected all fetishes, has become a fetish himself. Zazzle sells sweatshirts stamped with his face and emblazoned with the slogan "Nietzsche is Peachy." History is full of pranks.

"I am condemned," wrote Nietzsche, "to entertain the next eternity with bad jokes." In a time of endless reruns and recycled schlock, when Superman is a failing comic book franchise, pop stars sing "What doesn't kill you makes you stronger!" and academic conferences discuss the existential meaning of *Groundhog Day*, the German philosopher is doomed to be a punch line. Confronted with the concept of Eternal Recurrence, Woody Allen broods: "God—I'll have to sit through the Ice Capades again." But there is nothing ridiculous about Nietzsche's challenge to our superficial and passive generation, numbed by depression and indifference, addicted to glibness and irony, gluttonous for debasing entertainment: *If you could, would you live your life over again, exactly as it is? If not, do you have the courage to change it?*

VII

After Babel

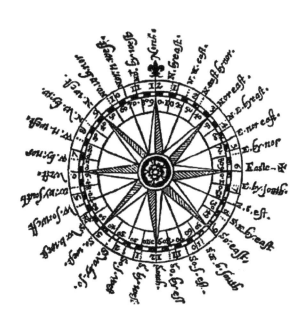

Andrei

Nonwords

> Little by little she became a word, bundles of soul on the wind.
> —Nichita Stănescu, "Sign 12"

THE ROMANIAN POET NICHITA STĂNESCU is generally acknowledged as one of the country's most popular, charismatic, and influential writers of the twentieth century. He has been called by literary critic Eugen Simion, "a great Romanian poet in an impossible history, the epoch of totalitarianism." At first these two terms—poet and totalitarianism—seem irreconcilable, and yet hardly anyone would criticize Stănescu for compromising his work in favor of ideology. He was, and remains, a skilled wordsmith, a champion of language—*poet* in the purest sense of the word.

Stănescu's early works, which earned him both national and international praise, were a product of the 1950s and '60s, a period when the arts generally flourished with little interference from the government as long as the content did not overtly attack the Communist Party or denounce its ideology. The latter part of his career, however, specifically the late '70s to his death in 1983, unfolded just as Romania was entering one of the most oppressive periods in its history. Nicolae Ceaușescu's grotesque personality cult had begun to put a stranglehold on freedom of expression.

Stănescu's writing, then, straddled not only a period of cultural liberalization and experimentation, but also one of stifling censorship when language and literature in Romania were restricted to the glorification of the Communist Party. At this time many classic works of literature were banned or, if they were made accessible, were edited to reflect party ideology. Content was removed that would potentially offend the leadership or damage public morale. Plays were barred from being staged. Writers were imprisoned and persecuted for their work. When Stănescu was nominated for the Nobel Prize, it was widely suspected that party sabotage prevented him from receiving the honor.

℃

The relatively "free" decade of Stănescu's early works notwithstanding, his aesthetics throughout his short but prolific career allow us to ask the broader question: How do artists create and exist within rigidly imposed structures of language and ideology without succumbing to rhetoric or glorifying abstract ideals contrary to the free spirit?

One way and possible answer offered by Stănescu's oeuvre is by reconstructing the world through language, poetic language, a space where the reorganization and redefinition of words preserves truth and makes it possible in the face of adversity. The beginning of such reorganization requires and happens through the destruction of an old language whose meaning is derived from tyrannically imposed signifiers. As such, it is always an act *against*.

"When at first I learned to speak, I used all my words to fight," sing the Avett Brothers in "I and Love and You." Even if ultimately history does not consider him a "political poet" per se, Stănescu's whole life was a primer of resistance. He was born in 1933 in Ploieşti, a city of oil refineries, to a Romanian peasant father and a Russian immigrant mother. His childhood was traumatized by war, his teenage years blighted by his country's abject adjustment to communism. After studying linguistics and literature in Bucharest, for the rest of his life Stănescu was obsessed with language, and he would learn to wield it with uncanny skill.

Stănescu's poems stand out as lyrical agents of resistance against conventional meaning when words become more than units of speech and enter the realm of objects—relics, talismans, weapons. Angela Leighton, in her book *On Form: Poetry, Aestheticism, and the Legacy of a Word*, accurately captures the intent and the culminating effect of a writer as conscious of language as Stănescu, and, in Leighton's example, Virginia Woolf:

Words, for Woolf, can have the poetic tangibility of solid objects. Her prose turns them over and over, till they ring unfamiliarly in the ear. She can thus, through repetition, make a word sound resistant and palpable, not a clear opening to sense which allows a meaning to pass, but thick with its own shape—indeed, *just* a word. Such words remain set against representation, their object to mess their object...and to call attention to themselves instead.

Language can be a coat of many colors or a white straightjacket in a mental asylum. It depends on who tailors our words. "When I use a word," Humpty Dumpty tells Alice, rather scornfully, "it means just what I choose it to mean—neither more nor less." The question is not whether words can be made to mean so many things but which is to be master. That's all. "We do not speak language," said Martin Heidegger; "language speaks us." For eggheads, this pronouncement is a call for papers; for poets, it is a call to arms.

Like Lewis Carroll's Alice, Stănescu invites us to step through the looking glass and defy the Red Queen. In the Wonderland of his imagination, metaphors beget strange verbal structures, unusual combinations of linguistic signs. Stănescu called these phenomena *nonwords*: semantic disturbances in the old order, ruptures in official discourse, grammars before grammar school. Precognitive and prelingual, *nonwords* are both intuitive and elusive. They lurk simultaneously beyond the realm of understanding and exist prior to the realization of meaning. As such, they have the singular capacity of subverting ideology. They are not gibberish but a secret code from the revolution of the unconscious.

Such writing is powerful and evocative precisely because by calling attention to the unique qualities of language it draws attention away from an all-encompassing and totalizing mentality, and locates agency at the moment of the individual's active engagement and struggle with meaning. Out of this arises a *new meaning* and therefore a *new logic* of the imagination that defies conventional logic. And because conventional logic overwhelmingly serves the state, artists, compelled by history and character, have always found ways to defy and circumvent censorship and say what they mean without drawing the ire of the establishment. It is in this way—by circumventing convention and ideology through a radical language of the imagination—that Stănescu the "metaphysical poet" might even be considered a "political poet" or at the very least a poet engaged in a political act.

❧

Mark Edmunson, who teaches poetry and Romanticism at the University of Virginia, draws the battle line in "The Ideal English Major," a polemical essay published in *The Chronicle of Higher Education*:

> What does it mean to be spoken by language? It means to be a vehicle for expression and not a shaper of words. It means to rely on clichés and preformulated expressions. It means to be a channeler, of ad-speak, sports jargon, and the latest psychological babble. You sound not like a living man or a woman but like something much closer to a machine, trying to pass for human. You never know how you feel or what you want in life because the words at your disposal are someone else's and don't represent who you are and what you want. You don't and can't know yourself. You don't and can't know the world.

> The businessman prattles about excellence, leadership, partnerships, and productivity. The athlete drones on about the game plan, the coach, one play at a time, and the inestimable blessing of having teammates who make it all possible. The politician pontificates about unity, opportunity, national greatness, and what's in it for the middle class. When such people talk, they are not so much human beings as tape loops.

Stănescu would have agreed. The enemy is prepackaged language, from totalitarian propaganda to moronically cheerful psychobabble. But this jabberwocky cannot be slain by directly challenging or clashing with authority. The dragon may be ridiculous, but its talons have a death grip on our culture and imagination. Instead, we must destroy language as we know it, as we expect it to be, and create a new cosmos of signs and signifiers. If we want to topple the Tower of Babel, then, we must speak in tongues. "To restore to words their full significance, as in dreams," said Norman O. Brown, "is to reduce them to nonsense, to get the nonsense or nothingness or silence back into words; to transcend the antinomy of sense and nonsense, silence and speech. It is a destruction of ordinary language, a victory over the reality principle."

Stănescu's control of language, and, further, his construction of radical metaphor that gave his poetry its own kind of lexicon, proves the resilience of language in the face of increasing tyranny and oppression of any kind—its ability to convey and celebrate universal human sentiments that transcend the limitations of ideology. Through a return to the *unfamiliar*, Nichita Stănescu's *nonwords* rescue readers from a world of farce and spectacle, of rigid dogma and blatant atrocity. By troubling an expected lexical paradigm they transported readers, however briefly, to a world of a hope, a country of the imagination with no borders and endless possibilities where rocks can fly, arrows are molded from tears, feathers wound, and the sky walks on its hind legs. He re-enchanted a disenchanted land whose leaders had sacrificed all beauty and magic to austerity, efficiency, and brutality. *"What loneliness to find no meaning when there is meaning,"* he said, *"and what loneliness to be blind in the full light of day, deaf amidst the swelling of a song."*

As the ideological noose tightened and expression in the arts became increasingly filled with party rhetoric, Stănescu continued to write on universally relevant topics such as the fate of humanity, the soul, and man's relationship to the world around him. As Alexandru Condeescu notes in his introduction to *Ordinea Cuvintelor* (*The Order of Words*), Stănescu "sought through the theater invented by him, where he was both actor and viewer, the revelation of The Truth." This truth, however, is ultimately not just metaphysical but existential. Like many before and after him, Stănescu honored language's potential to create an alternate reality.

What, then, is more political that the act and ability to speak freely in a time of censorship or to express oneself and one's ideas outside of an imposed and curated linguistic regime? Stănescu refused to use words as they had been used when coerced into service. And by replacing controlled, objective discourse with anarchic, subjective wordplay, Stănescu freed his thinking and writing and inspired others to do the same. He offered his readers freedom of the mind, the unconditional love of language, and maybe even a sliver of Truth.

Instructions for Learning a New Language

Disassemble the furniture of joy, the two uneasy beds of a youthful heart, false lives and the poverty of hope, gently pull at the ancient nail and wood construction, the furniture of lies, small and giant boxes and loopholes, the passed down furniture of marriage and old age, warm hearted chambers of forgotten years, those woolen bolts of happiness, love's propaganda, posters for the always wanting to be beautiful, undressed and violently beautiful, windblown into a million bits and pieces, into itch of dust, cry in the throat, night of disconnected dreams, dark bells and muddy water spitting through the iron mouths of boulevards, rain of urban iridescent yellow, splash of the harbor, the static cling of loud skirts and short blouses, new windows, not enough storage space, not enough, not enough, and our shelves heavy and creaking with old coffee cans full of broken zippers and buttons.

Anatomy of Dreams

I took a class once on the anatomy of dreams. Our assignments consisted of making something out of nothing, which is harder than it sounds. I renounced all I had, this illegible, broken alphabet that has nearly broken me. I slept through the whole thing, whittled my nights in the shape of petrified birds. One drinks still from the bowl of old milk at the head of the table, the only color and shape we were allowed to give to the passage of time. That bird, I like to believe, is the happiest of the unfortunate lot. Some shattered, heavy as the thoughts that gave them a name, and still others, lighter than a single word with all its hollow chambers, took flight and disappeared. On some days, hardly noticeable ripples, I find myself sitting at the table, across from the one who's yet to drink one drop, waiting for it to begin whispering to me, to tell me what it wants.

Encoded

I dressed silence in the image of my father. It came dressed inside the image of a heavy bird, a milky tongue, the dog that watches me until I'm out of sight. I buried its familiar face inside the flowerbeds on autumn's street inside the silver paintings water fountains wet cement the copper monuments electric blues and violins. It came out as a loaf of bread the rotting garbage in the street a young girl wearing too much on her face. There's no way out of it. The magic fails eventually. We become dissonant chords. The women in prophetic red turn out to be just women, my father turns into an old man overnight. A lifetime and we still don't know the many coats of silence. Rust that pricks the tender eye, a tear that trips over what vanishes . . . an impossibly long list. We are somewhere on there, calloused heels and broken skin. Smudges of dark lead, typewriter ink. One day we walked right off the page and could not find our way back.

Antonio

Dreams of a Common Language (Pt. 1)

DURING THE RISORGIMENTO, when a handful of idealists tried to fashion a seamless democracy from a patchwork of squabbling duchies, patriots sought national identity in classic literature. If Italians could relearn the language of Dante and Petrarch, the language of Renaissance Florence, Italy's greatest city-state, they could relearn the meaning of freedom and recover their pride.

This proposition—more convincing in the polite hush of Milanese salons than in the sarcastic uproar of Roman coffee-houses—had one flaw. The language of Renaissance Florence was as dead as Etruscan. Only the literati read it. Worse, nobody spoke its modern offshoot, best suited for barter and gossip, outside of Tuscany. The rest of Italy was a Babel of tongues. Piedmont's House of Savoy conducted diplomacy in French, love affairs in Turinese. The Bourbon court at Caserta cracked jokes in Neapolitan. Vatican prelates recited the mass in Latin but delivered sermons and ordered tripe in Romanesco. Merchants, lawyers, and gondoliers on the Rialto haggled, quibbled, and crooned in Venetian.

Italy would never be united as a country, nationalists claimed, until it was united in language. This Herculean task fell not to a bold revolutionary but to a timid scribbler, a man who preferred libraries to barricades and stammered in public. His name was Alessandro Manzoni, a minor aristocrat and nineteenth-century Italy's most beloved author, doomed to become required reading in a repressive public school system.

Don Alessandro was a paradox. Born in Milan on March 7, 1785, he was the grandson of the jurist and political scientist Cesare Beccaria, whose treatise *On Crimes and Punishment* (1764) abolished torture and amended the death penalty in Europe and America. Weaned on the skepticism and classicism of the French Enlightenment, Manzoni later converted to Catholicism and Romanticism. As a scholar and a writer, he professed a mystical nationalism.

Manzoni's poetry sang of political and spiritual unity. "March 1821," a civic ode, exhorts Italians to form a single nation: "*una d'arme, di lingua, d'altare*," one in arms, tongue, and faith. "Pentecost," the most beautiful of his *Sacred Hymns* (1822), presents a biblical vision of liberty, equality, and fraternity. As different colors are merely the subjective impressions of the sun's cosmic light, different languages are only the incidental expressions of God's universal mind. With tongues of flame, the Holy Spirit proclaims a new era of freedom and justice to the world's emerging nations.

It was Manzoni's prose, however, that midwifed the birth of Italy. *The Betrothed* (1827), a historical novel inspired by Sir Walter Scott, denounced foreign domination and mocked corrupt institutions. Expressing the two sides of Manzoni's personality, his Voltairean irony and Franciscan piety, this homely epic about life's nobodies became the primer of the Risorgimento.

Set in seventeenth-century Milan under Spanish rule, *The Betrothed* centers on Renzo and Lucia, an engaged peasant couple from Lombardy's Lake District, whose wedding plans are thwarted by a petty tyrant. Separated by war, famine, and plague, the two reunite and start a home. The novel is not only a panorama of a fascinating period of Italian history but also a meditation on power and language. Renzo and Lucia, both illiterate, are bullied and bamboozled by the parish priest's catechism, the lawyer's contract, the police spy's notebook, and the governor's edicts. Until they learn how to read and write, Manzoni implies, they cannot be free.

This theme appealed to Northern liberals, many of whom were journalists and educators. They embraced *The Betrothed*, calling it an allegory on Austrian occupation. The novel converted people to the cause of unification, but not everyone was pleased. Giuseppe Mazzini, founder of Young Italy, complained that the book was too domestic. "Its joys are the joys of family," he growled; "its sufferings do not lead to revolt." Luigi Settembrini, the Neapolitan republican, complained that it advocated Christian resignation, not civic engagement. Others criticized its incoherent politics and patronizing depiction of peasants and artisans, who were hardly heroic. But the book's lack of an overt agenda and its humorous characters appeased the censors and attracted middle-class readers.

The first edition sold out in ten weeks. More printings followed, but Manzoni discovered that supply could not meet demand. During a trip to Pisa and Florence, customers mobbed the stores. To secure copyright against pirates, Manzoni commissioned an illustrated edition, which proved even more popular. The novel's unprecedented success, at home and abroad, fed academic and public debates about Italy's language question.

Encouraged by colleagues, Manzoni decided to revise *The Betrothed*. He would translate his novel's somewhat bookish Lombard into conversational Tuscan. This painstaking task took thirteen years. Manzoni described this process as *"risciacquare i panni in Arno,"* rinsing his laundry in the Arno. On field trips to Florence, he loitered in shops and eavesdropped in cafés. He read drafts aloud to his children's Tuscan governess to perfect a genuine vernacular style. When academics objected, Manzoni tartly reminded them that Dante, "who had been a man and not a marble bust," wrote in the language of cobblers.

The revised novel, published in 1842, became an instant classic. It went through more than seventy editions and reprints and sold a quarter of a million copies—an astonishing figure given the limited size of Italy's reading public. Nationalists were delighted. For the first time, foreign critics compared an Italian author to Balzac, Cooper, and Dickens. The book had focused international attention on unification and had strengthened the cause of standardization. Much work, however, remained. This was evident when the Kingdom of Italy was formed in 1861.

At the time, only 2.5 percent of the population (630,000 out of a total of 25 million people) was fluent in the Italian now used in the nation's public institutions. These were mostly native Tuscans and bureaucrats from Piedmont and Lombardy. If one included children who had been exposed to official Italian in secondary school, this figure might rise to 10 percent. For the 80 percent of the population classified as illiterate, however, Italian remained a foreign language, not only in Naples and Palermo, where it was practically incomprehensible, but even in Venice and Rome. If Italy was ever to achieve its dream of a common language, the state must resort to stricter methods.

Andrei

Palimpsest

If it were that easy to be reborn. Broken down reformed and gleaming like a thumb-worn stone upon the breastbone. Unwritten skin, snow before mud. In this unnatural city, this impossible flesh that parts to let you slide in, faceless with a heartbeat. Dear Beloved, if it were that easy, we would all be the children of stars, unblemished, sitting around the table, wise with the wine. We would smell of bread and the warm breath of fire, of the ground after a summer rain. Enough. That would be enough. But the moon here is oblivious of your absence. The flag is even more oblivious of your grief. You are devoured the moment that you open your mouth, you disappear in the bloodswell of old eyes going soft inside their cages. You are the still frame in a movie that no one has dreamed about yet. You are also not a window of hatred or love or the irrational philosophies of dying men. And for that you do not get a name. You, bearer of the single life, there is another shoulder propped beneath your burden. It also doesn't have a name.

Under Our Fingernails

What more can I say about certain places and the weary night song piled outside every window? It can weigh you down like happiness, like a steady rain, like the notion of destiny or an obligatory farewell that you carry strapped to your shoulders.

Believe me, if it would help you see things in a different light I would only write about ballerinas and playgrounds of improbable laughter. The sun and the ubiquitous fresh air added to every scene would do you a world of good. And I would make it rain softly, just enough to spruce up the flowers. I would do all of this in a countryside dialect and part my hair accordingly to resemble a soft smile.

But the truth is I could never understand why a single language is not enough for us. A simple breath blown into an empty bottle and tossed into the nearest stream, something everyone knows how to interpret. Instead we suffer through this all-too-human need for a philosophy of words when a howl would do much better. Let's leave behind the fancy embroidery—we are but stray dogs missing the fancy leash and the tinderbox of home we sometimes call a house.

(

Places change because through the years we change even less. We've spent too much time in the dirt and now everything is relative to and because of it. More or less under our fingernails. Scrape away then rinse repeat and still the hounding scent and memory of evenings spent under the stars, our backs on the ground and nothing but a long sigh for a sheet to pull up to the neck. How many sighs does it take to resemble a death? To make this place fold into another, then another...

Let's begin counting now and see who gets there first. *Ce n'est pas le cirque du soleil.* That much any fool could tell you for a nickel. Just open your eyes when the night peaks at its most exotic and serious black. We've been here before, you and I. Surrounded by sounds that would never make sense out of context. But there was no need to translate what the crickets said. For once there was no need.

Wordless

There are times when one word traveling in a straight line from one mouth to another bends around light and forgets where it was going, pauses in the grass on the banks of the river and contemplates carving out a wave, dipping its toes in the mist—still waiting, the mouth on the other side calls in despair, not in language, not anything intelligible, but it gets caught in the trees, its shirt is torn, it throws up its hands and sky goes white in surrender—white of the daydreamers' plume, white of November's first fire made solely for watching—wordless, meaning bound to the bone—how the body enters into knowing—wordless— how the deepest mark will search eternally for tongues on which to rest its blame.

Antonio

Dreams of a Common Language (Pt. 2)

WHEN ALESSANDRO MANZONI agreed to chair the language committee, the Minister of Education celebrated with a bottle of Carpano vermouth. The old man's *imprimatur* would win public support for this project and legitimize the government's final report. If only Governor d'Azeglio had lived to see this moment! He would have honored his father-in-law's appointment with a panegyric in the Senate.

Now eighty-two years old, Manzoni was a living monument. In his native Milan, he attracted nearly as many tourists as the city's bristly cathedral. The Chamber of Commerce had coined a slogan: "*Un tempio ed un uomo: Manzoni ed il Duomo!*" Verdi and Garibaldi, Cardinal Newman and Prime Minister Gladstone, Henry Wadsworth Longfellow and Emperor Pedro of Brazil made pilgrimages to his three-storied palazzo on Via Morone. Beneath the octagonal dome of the Galleria Vittorio Emanuele, Milan's unfinished glassed arcade, bookshops sold lithographs of him like holy cards.

Don Alessandro was considered a saint. Slight and stooped, he wore black frock coats, spoke in a gentle quaver, and was as humble as a country rector. His aquiline nose, sunken cheeks, and thin muttonchops would have made him severe, if it had not been for a pair of twinkling hazel eyes and a nimbus of white hair. He put a kind face on state cruelty.

The language committee formed in January 1868. Within days, Manzoni drafted a proposal. Linguistic centralization, it argued, was needed to complement political unity. Grammar and usage, syntax and style must reinforce national identity. State schools should impose Florentine Italian and stigmatize regional dialects. Textbooks should be standardized. Teachers should be recruited only from Tuscany. Anthologies should be purged of all dialect literature.

This draconian plan appalled Graziadio Isaia Ascoli, the Jewish philologist, who pleaded for dialects to be respected. Any standardization of Italian should be allowed to occur spontaneously as communication and culture gradually spread. This process already was happening. Soldiers and civil servants recruited from all over the peninsula were introducing regional words and idioms into official Italian. *Ciao*, for example, a northern greeting and parting derived from the Venetian phrase *s-ciào su* (your slave or servant), was catching on in central and southern cities.

But the Ministry of Education was adamant. No sacrifice was too great for linguistic unity! Niccolò Tommaseo, the Dalmatian essayist, went blind preparing the first standard Italian dictionary. Carlo Goldoni's Venetian comedies, Giovanni Meli's Sicilian poems, and Giuseppe Belli's Roman satires were banished from Parnassus. By purifying the Italian language, the state would purify the Italian race.

The government targeted illiterate Southerners, whom educated Northerners considered black. "We did not unite Italy," they complained. "We divided Africa." The Mezzogiorno, the former territory of the Kingdom of the Two Sicilies, remained a hotbed of crime and rebellion. Troops had failed to restore order and to integrate the region into the country. Schools might succeed. If Southern children were made as white as the pages of a composition book, they would assimilate and become productive citizens in a liberal democracy.

Classrooms were hell. Children were humiliated, beaten, and expelled for refusing to read *The Betrothed*. Manzoni's son-in-law Giovanni Battista Giorgini, an Italian senator and a professor at the Scuola Normale di Pisa, had enshrined the text in public schools. Teachers were baffled and offended. How could these pickaninnies reject the book that had made Italy?

Few recognized the irony. Manzoni had liberated the vernacular from academics. Now academics used him to imprison the vernacular of half the country. Manzoni had dignified *la gente senza storia*, the poor and anonymous masses ignored by official history. Under his aegis, however, officials denied the dignity and erased the history of Southern

Italians. Sicilians never forgave this Milanese Prospero for capturing their island with a strange book or for teaching generations of little Calibans to curse in a strange tongue. A million left.

Manzoni regretted these abuses and struggled to overcome his ambivalence toward *terroni*, Southern dirt farmers. They were the salt of the earth but better fit perhaps for the Kingdom of God than the Kingdom of Italy. Manzoni never denied his own Southern heritage. His maternal grandmother had been a noblewoman of Sicilian stock. He conceded that Sicilians had invented the Italian sonnet and had influenced Dante. But when he encountered Sicilian migrants in the Piazza del Duomo, wearing bandanas and earrings and conversing in what sounded like Arabic, he crossed himself. He feared that the cathedral spires would turn into minarets. "*Così fatto è questo guazzabuglio del cuore umano*," he sighed. Such is the muddle of the human heart.

The man who united his nation by uniting its language led a divided life. Outwardly, Manzoni played the witty and serene if melancholy sage. Inwardly, he mourned the death of two wives and seven children and suffered panic attacks. He shrank from puddles. Cheeping sparrows set his teeth on edge. Thunderstorms frightened and crowds terrified him. Strict routine controlled his anxiety. He attended morning mass, lunched on broth, weighed his clothes to ensure that they were thick enough for the chill, and took walks. Not long ago, he could hike the Dugnani Public Gardens or stroll along the Naviglio Grande. Now, he barely managed the historic district near his home. The construction and shopping menaced him. Buildings swayed, sidewalks cracked. Pedestrians in the Galleria Mall trampled him.

On January 6, 1873, the Feast of the Epiphany, Manzoni was observing the architectural restoration of his parish church, San Fedele. Leaving for home, he slipped on some ice and hit his head on the steps. The concussion swelled his brain. For five months, he flitted in and out of consciousness. Delirium alternated with flashes of wit. When a nurse asked him why he was so addled, Don Alessandro replied: "If I knew, I wouldn't be addled, would I?" After receiving the last rites, he died on May 22, Ascension Thursday, and was laid in Palazzo Marino, City Hall. The lavish state funeral would have embarrassed the old man.

Shops were closed, memorial odes taped in the windows and pasted on the walls. Mourners packed the streets from Piazza della Scala to the Cimitero Monumentale. A squadron of cavalry and a delegation of scholastics preceded the bier, drawn by six black horses. Princes Umberto and Amedeo of the House of Savoy carried the flanking cords. The presidents of the Senate and the Chamber and the ministers of education and foreign affairs assisted. Papers published empty elegies. "Many words," said Giuseppe Verdi, "but none deeply felt." As a proper tribute, he composed a requiem in Manzoni's honor. Music alone speaks directly to the heart.

Manzoni's dream of a common language was fulfilled after World War II. During the boom, national broadcasting reconquered the Mezzogiorno. Laborers came north and worked at Pirelli and Alfa Romeo. Both trends popularized standard Italian but never united Italy. During the Sesquicentennial of the Risorgimento, separatists disrupted national celebrations. Lega Nord renewed its efforts to found Padania, an independent state stretching from Val d'Aosta to Emilia-Romagna. The Patrioti Napolitani Briganti demanded the restoration of the Bourbon monarchy. The Sicilian Independence Movement dogged the Regional Assembly. Protestors called for the teaching of regional dialects in public schools. *"Fuck the fatherland!"* they chanted. *"Speak your mother tongue!"*

Italy's immigration crisis fueled this identity crisis. Boat people flooding Lampedusa, mostly refugees from rebellions in Tunisia and Libya, were considered an invading armada. Declaring a state of emergency, Prime Minister Silvio Berlusconi dispatched armed troops to round up North African and Eastern European illegals. This action encouraged public backlash. Campo de' Fiori, Rome's crossroads of the nations, an international market where Arabic, Congolese, Hindi, and Romani are spoken, experienced race riots. Nativist gangs clubbed and stabbed immigrant merchants. Similar violence occurred in Turin and Milan. Tensions ran highest after soccer games because some players are first- or second-generation African Italians. Heckling Kevin-Prince Boateng, skinheads at Verona's Bentegodi Stadium threw bananas and grunted like apes: "Oo—oo—oo—oo!"

Italy's survival, however, depends on its immigrants, who are teaching their adopted country a new language. Karima, a Liberian Italian rapper, combats racism in music videos. Amara Lakhous, an Algerian Italian novelist, won the Flaiano Prize for *Clash of Civilization over an Elevator in Piazza Vittorio*, a satire on xenophobia. "*Io arabizzo l'italiano e italianizzo l'arabo*," he explains. "I Arabize Italian and Italianize Arabic." Cécile Kyenge, Italy's first black minister, is a dignified public speaker. "I am proud to be an Italian," she declares, despite being called "an orangutan" by Robert Calderoli, Vice President of the Northern League. "A cultural shift is taking place in this country, especially among the young."

Pope Francis I attributes this awakening global consciousness to the Holy Spirit. The son of immigrant Italian parents, the former Archbishop of Buenos Aires believes that the West's salvation lies with the Third World. If democracy is to be more than a word, more than a fig leaf for greed and arrogance, then prosperous nations must welcome the poor and dispossessed. Unity must be based on diversity, justice on equality. To support this argument, Papa Francesco quotes his favorite author, Alessandro Manzoni, who prayed for Pentecost in the midst of Babel:

> O prevailing Spirit, come
> To Thy solemn altars! We,
> Hermits in a forest home,
> Wanderers on the lonely sea,
> From Lebanon to Andes hoar,
> From Erin's green to stark Haiti,
> Scattered over every shore,
> Joined into one heart by Thee,
> We implore Thee!

VIII

What's So Real about Surrealism?

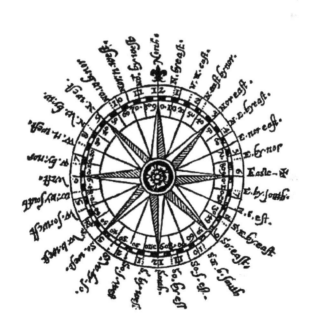

Andrei

Funny When You Think about It

DURING THE 1980S, UNDER NICOLAE CEAUŞESCU, daily life in Romania resembled an ironic version of the *Divine Comedy*, with Emil Cioran, Mircea Eliade, and Eugène Ionesco as a compound Virgil and family members as Sapia and Cacciaguida, Lucia and Beatrice. More than Florence, Bucharest contained all of the circles of Hell, Purgatory, and Heaven. At the very least, this ordeal taught one to tolerate their earthly equivalent, an all-too-human theater of the absurd. In many ways, both explicitly and implicitly, Ceauşescu's surreal regime haunts both the Eastern and Western imagination, and has come to define not only my own work but to a large extent that of other Romanian writers of my generation. How could it not? In the winter there was no heat, no hot water, and cooking gas was available for one hour beginning at midnight. Think of an entire nation standing around stoves well past midnight to cook rice and beans, shaved bones for a bit of flavor. Such are the tragicomic snapshots from my album of childhood memories. Some mysterious Kodak carousel projects these often bizarre images on the screen of my writing. Nothing seems to capture those years, the sentiments of my country, better than the absurd. How else can one explain the grotesqueness of the Ceauşescu years?

Palatul Parlamentului, the Palace of Parliament, is the world's largest and most expensive functioning administrative building. Begun in 1983, its construction required the demolition of much of Bucharest's historic district, including nineteen Orthodox Christian churches, six Jewish synagogues, three Protestant churches, and thirty thousand residences. Even Nero destroyed less of Rome to build the *Domus Aurea* on the Palatine Hill. According to the *Guinness Book of World Records*, the palace includes one million cubic meters of marble from Transylvania, most from Ruşchiţa; 3,500 tons of crystal for 480 chandeliers,

1,409 ceiling lights and hundreds of mirrors; 700,000 tons of steel and bronze for monumental doors and windows, candelabra and capitals; 9,700,000 square feet of wood, over 95 percent domestic, for parquet and wainscoting, including walnut, oak, sweet cherry, elm, sycamore maple; 2,200,000 square feet of woolen carpets of various dimensions. The larger were woven on-site by machines moved into the building. The velvet and brocade curtains are adorned with embroideries and passementeries in silver and gold.

Ceauşescu called this monstrosity *Casa Poporului*, the People's House. Meanwhile, in urban slums and rural hovels, the rest of the country starved and ratted each other out behind closed doors. At the time of Ceauşescu's 1989 overthrow and execution, the palace's structure and design were complete, but most of the furniture was never installed. Many rooms are still empty, while the last three basement levels and a large clock tower (which would display the official Romanian time) remain unfinished. The same is true of parts of the west wing, the east wing, and the second floor. In this tale of waste and folly, laughter meets the painfully real, the strikingly vivid. Is it any wonder that Tristan Tzara and Dadaism both have their roots in Romania?

According to Costica Bradatan, editor of *Philosophy, Society and the Cunning of History in Eastern Europe*, Eastern Europeans have a genius for marrying surreal humor with harsh reality. For generations, this strategy has ensured daily survival. "Caught between empires, often marked by catastrophic historic events and grand political failures, the countries of East-Central Europe have for a long time developed a certain intellectual self-representation," Bradatan states, "a culture that not only helps them make some sense of such misfortunes, but also protects them somehow from a collapse into nihilism."

This self-representation is fraught with complications, since, as Bradatan writes, East Europeans "are not exactly comfortable with who, or what, they are. As a matter of fact, it may well be that this very sense of metaphysical discomfort, this incapacity to come up with, and accept, a firm self-definition, is one of the main character traits of East Europeans, something that 'defines' them in the end."

This sly and sophisticated philosophy of adaption and endurance, in which precariousness is a virtue and skepticism a tonic, counterbalances a history of religious and political martyrdom, collective suffering, and geopolitical fatalism. After all, Bradatan adds:

> [W]hat makes Eastern Europeans uncomfortable is the inescapable feeling that they were born "in the wrong place," "at the wrong time," or both. [Czeslaw] Milosz, who knew about these things only too well, regards East Europeans as being "burdened with a longing for a homeland other than the one assigned from birth." It would not even be accurate to say that East European identity is defined by *dislocation*. It is much worse than that: it is an identity defined by a most uncanny form of nostalgia: *nostalgia* for deracination, a compulsive need for losing one's roots, but without the prospect of growing new roots elsewhere.

The secret to the perseverance of entire generations caught in such a historical and self-induced limbo is abiding in existential and political contradictions. Even now, more than a quarter century after the fall of the Iron Curtain, one is struck by a paradox—lingering sadness about the past coupled with the reckless, even joyful abandon of progress. Tragic, yes, but that's life, and it has the stink of the inevitable. At least that's how Bradatan characterizes Eastern Europeans' attitude towards their historical reality: "[W]hat seems to distinguish East Europeans' perception of their misfortunes is the *character of permanence*. For the Eastern European, historical disasters not only happen, they do so on a regular basis; they keep happening so stubbornly that their occurrence ceases to be seen as accidental and becomes part and parcel of life."

And because it has the appearance of comfort and normality, ultimately it gets us no further than a theory of circumstance taken up by generation after generation of armchair philosophers and "I-told-you-so's." Meanwhile, to preserve appearances, politicians bicker and fight as if parliament is a daytime soap opera and citizens for the most part go along for the ride. Twenty-five years, and no one knows yet whether the revolution was a sham; few even seem to care.

Centuries, and we still do not know who we are. We move forward while standing still. Indeed, what more can one do in the face of history? The Romanian shrugs and says, "It can always be worse," then pours a drink and finds something to laugh about. In the end it's the only thing that makes any sense.

Even Though Everyone Knows Better

A single drop of blood goes unnoticed, as do the black stains of motor oil, the butane fingertips. In the pure night that extends beyond the city crown only sounds make it through—the plastic crawl of the clock, the rooster's stupid loyalty to a sun that no longer cares what it burns. That simple dog that begets more simple dogs and their howls of honest suffering.

☾

So much racket and the streets so empty at this hour. Black head matches piled on by the millions and still no shred of flame! Only blind talk everywhere, schoolyard threats and peacock feathers. Loud-talkers and the ones who don't give a damn about being saved because that will not happen in our lifetime. I guess that I'm here for that, too. That weak white spot of reason on the margins of imagination.

☾

That drop of blood goes unnoticed and a thousand more follow, but they are also all just single drops. What can you do, anyway? Stay up counting the infinite? Take a seat at the table with the fortunate lot and blow smoke over all of it—we'll die of this and look good doing it. Drink to that and find yourself a woman who still wants to have children. Drink to that, too, out of sheer happiness.

Without a Hero

On two moonlit horses we galloped toward the outer boroughs, evening's roots pushing the salty sky down our throats. We were done naming clouds and now turned our attention to the muddy rooftops, the ash and smoke of effigies we built just so we would have something to burn. When the rain came it trembled on our brows, soaked us to the waist. Our wasted bodies glimmered like a thousand crazy eyes, like the swelling of blood in a pool in the courtyard where dreams go to await their awakening. The night became wet with our voices calling through the mist. We called out and a bird answered, or a dog looking for his master, or the horn of a distant ship dragging the day through the waters. We mounted our horses again and kicked at their ribs full with worms and dry grass. We coughed smoke, bit down on the swollen tongue of the city—shattering, always shattering. Burning skyward like a field of poppies.

It Ends Differently

In every dream a tapestry of doors swings open to a bowl of buckwheat sewing steam into the frigid air. The countermen have wide bellies and the salesgirls grovel behind starch heavy aprons. Annotated smiles is all they have time for. Obligations handed down as a dead man's request, a last hiss from the hull of the body, impossible to ignore.

In every dream the hired holy carry the cross in one hand, a dagger in the other. Indoctrination at every level. They blow Sunday kisses to the seraphim when the envelope drops with a hush into the wicker basket. Stuck under your very nose!

Such tender, lucid moments wedged into the ragged dusk by a million prayers. Grooves cut deep as a fishbone in the mouth. And the smell of camphor like an echo through the hallways where the injured morning is licking her wounds. There was promise in that first hour, and then...

But maybe it doesn't have to end that way. In every dream the haze of daylight leans on your very doorstep. There is always that. And those who would lead an old man by the arm, patting the bony wrist, taking turns at the soapbox of idealism. Anything that might keep us moving on. Small needs that no bullet can penetrate. A kind word or two flung through the distance.

Antonio

The Disquieting Muses (Pt. 1)

To HONOR THE THIRTIETH ANNIVERSARY of Giorgio de Chirico's death, the Museo Piaggio in Pontedera held a retrospective in the summer of 2008. The setting could not have been more fitting. Visitors could puzzle over such paintings as *The Enigma of the Hour, The Nostalgia of the Infinite,* and *The Melancholy and Mystery of a Street,* and also meander through exhibits of antique railway carriages, bomber fuselages, and early Vespas. De Chirico would have been delighted.

The son of a Sicilian railroad engineer, who had emigrated to Greece, de Chirico was as fascinated by modern industrial design as he was by classical architecture. Trained as a draughtsman at the Athens Polytechnic Institute, he pursued a career in Europe, where he studied German philosophy and explored Italian factories. His favorite city was Turin, whose vast squares and crooked arcades had driven Nietzsche mad. Responding to the shock of modernity in the years leading up to World War I, he created dreamscapes of the modern metropolis, at once beautiful and alienating. He also predicted the brutal and kitschy nightmare of Fascism, from which Italy has never fully awakened.

An epiphany inspired de Chirico's paintings. "One clear autumn afternoon," he later recalled, "I was sitting on a bench in the middle of the Piazza Santa Croce in Florence. It was of course not the first time I had seen this square. The whole world, down to the marble of the buildings and fountains, seemed to me to be convalescent. Then I had the strange impression I was looking at these things for the first time."

Every corner, every corbel, every column, de Chirico realized, possessed a spirit, an impenetrable soul. Every window gazed at him with mysterious, questioning eyes. The statue of Dante in front of the Basilica of Santa Croce, the Temple of Italian Glories where so many artists and statesmen were buried, seemed on the verge of coming to life.

The waning sun bathed everything in a strange glow. Silence and calm reigned supreme. Words could not express this enigma, only images.

De Chirico founded an avant-garde school called *pittura metafisica* (metaphysical art). Unlike the Futurists, who rejected history, de Chirico loved Italy's faded classical grandeur. He sought, therefore, to capture the dislocation between past and present. De Chirico's sense of time owed much to the French philosopher Henri Bergson. For the ancient Greeks and Romans, time was cyclical. For modern Europeans, it was linear. Once aboard the train of history, there was no getting off until the final station. All human yearning and sadness come from the perpetual disappearance of the present. We cannot hold time still no matter how hard we try. All things glide unstoppably into the past, where they can never be retrieved, only imperfectly remembered.

De Chirico, however, was a scientist as well as a mystic. Einstein had taught him that time was irrevocably related to space. Accordingly, he explored the dislocation between human subjects and the space they inhabit. His hallucinatory style results from irrational perspective, the lack of a unified light source, and the elongation of shadows. Bounded by arcades or classical façades, ordinary Italian piazzas are transformed into ominously silent and vacant settings for invisible dramas. These disjunctions in time and space provoke anxiety and nostalgia.

De Chirico's eerie cityscapes remove ordinary figures and objects from their familiar contexts to reveal inner life and meaning. Buildings, monuments, trains, smokestacks, sunglasses and mannequins are juxtaposed in bizarre associations. Prominent urban landmarks—Ferrara's Castello Estense, Milan's Galleria Vittorio Emanuele, Rome's Tempietto di San Pietro in Montorio, Turin's Mole Antonelliana—become signposts in the *Twilight Zone*. Submitted for our approval, even ordinary biscuits are imbued with occult meaning, communion wafers in a world haunted by the death of God.

De Chirico speaks in the symbolic language of dreams. Like a demented fortuneteller, he lays out vivid and bizarre cards and forms occult patterns on a flat table. Statues of classical goddesses or equestrian officers are truncated or hidden in growing shadows. Outskirts touch the edge of vast, inhospitable deserts, but the city itself is desolate. Streets are empty, arcades abandoned. Nobody loiters, strolls, or browses. Perhaps everyone is taking a siesta. Perhaps they are going crazy behind closed doors.

Or perhaps they are hiding from a dictator.

Andrei

Fraţii Mei (My Brothers)

On a mattress in the middle of a room I rock and cradle each premeasured gram of the daily bread. My hands have identical lifelines, which is only statistically impossible. I sit Buddha-style, Indian-style, I sit like a child, like a well-manicured doll. From this vantage point I dole out crumbs to the innocent but lately there are very few takers.

The brothers I never had also practice obscure rituals of self-preservation. One is unloading his worldly possessions for the benefit of the neighborhood poor. The other is bleaching medals for the day someone comes by to ask about their inherent value. Each one comes with a funny anecdote that he rehearses in the bathroom mirror.

We give what we have because we cannot give enough of ourselves. At all of our imaginary reunions there are many beautiful empty boxes. Barely enough room on the table for the perfect meal. We give so that we could finally leave something behind. At the end of the night, only one of us walks away lighter than the day before.

We head home in different directions, and tired, fall asleep dreaming of spiders.

Arrangement for Stills

At the table with the soup and the bread one fish eye looks back at me from the cage of its bones. It is too warm for soup but they insisted. The vinyl is painted with someone's interpretation of flowers and dirtied by the sun. It sticks to the bare skin of the arms angled as if meeting for prayer but stopped short by an afterthought.

Instructions have it that a spoon must be held in the right hand just so between the first and second finger, thumb gently resting on the handle. There is no knife and no fork because the artist's vision didn't call for them. There is a light at forty-five degrees, harsh but falling like cream from a pitcher on the face and shoulders. A small bird scatters from the trees and comes nearby to watch. I can only see it briefly from the corner of one eye because that's the way I've been arranged.

When the flash bursts the small bird scatters again, carrying light in its wings.

A Common Thing

You pause inside the belly of a country house, a knitted fly on the wall slowly coming undone. Someone hands you their first born, a flesh wound—not enough to make the world come to a halt. In your palm the swaddling cloth and the warmth freely given. The purled eyes never blink. Outside beyond fence and frost the sweetness leaks around the edges of an old moon shedding skin. When you leave by the back door notice how crowded a house without mirrors. The attic light falling on floor and boxes, aged barometers of mutual desire, twice cancelled and still to be paid for.

Antonio

The Disquieting Muses (Pt. 2)

"I WANT TO MAKE MY LIFE A MASTERPIECE," Benito Mussolini told Emil
Ludwig. Like Stendhal in the Basilica of Santa Croce, the German jour-
nalist and biographer of Napoleon swooned. He was not alone. Before
his atrocities in Ethiopia and pacts with Franco and Hitler alienated
and antagonized England and America, the Italian dictator inspired
something like *hyperkulturemia*, the psychosomatic disorder that causes
rapid heartbeat, dizziness, fainting, confusion and even hallucinations
when sufferers are exposed to great art.

Few were immune to Il Duce's charisma. Sigmund Freud and Carl
Jung, H. L. Mencken and G. K. Chesterton, Thomas Edison and Mahatma Gandhi considered him a Renaissance man, a cross between
Castiglione's courtier and Machiavelli's prince. With his flashing eyes,
jutting jaw, and barrel chest, he even resembled Verrocchio's equestrian statue of the *condottiero* Bartolomeo Colleoni in Venice's Campo
SS Giovanni e Paolo. Mussolini, however, compared himself to Mi-
chelangelo. He was not a politician, he said. He was a painter, sculptor,
and architect.

"What a man!" Winston Churchill gushed in a fan letter. "I have
lost my heart! Fascism has rendered a service to the entire world! If I
were Italian, I am sure I would have been with you entirely from the
beginning!"

Mussolini never would have come to power or inspired such fa-
natical devotion if he had merely drained swamps or improved train
schedules. After the carnage of World War I, Mussolini promised to
resurrect his country's glorious past. Only fifty years old in 1920, the
Kingdom of Italy had never cured itself of a chronic inferiority complex.
During the years preceding the Risorgimento (the Italian unification

movement), Rome's imperial ruins inspired shame, not pride. "O my country!" lamented Giacomo Leopardi, "I see the walls, arches, columns, statues, and lone towers of our ancestors, but not the glory!"

Mussolini exploited this shame. "A nation of spaghetti eaters," he scolded, "cannot restore Roman civilization!" What Italy required, he said, in harangue after harangue from the balcony of the Palazzo Venezia, was "a man who has when needed the heavy hand of a warrior and the delicate touch of an artist." Government, he said, could not function without the arts. Like Lorenzo de Medici, he befriended writers and painters, sculptors and composers, actors, and dancers. Every morning, he bragged, before leaving Villa Torlonia for the office, he would start the day with a bowl of grapefruit and a canto of Dante. Both were essential to good health.

Mussolini's totalitarian aestheticism was hardly new. During the fourteenth century, Cola di Rienzo's spellbinding rhetoric and hallucinatory stagecraft briefly revived the Roman Republic. Mussolini, however, was more ambitious than his predecessor. "In five years' time," he proclaimed in 1925, "Rome must astonish the peoples of the world. It must appear vast, orderly and powerful as it was in the days of Augustus." The best he could do was to turn the Eternal City into a dreamscape. Fascist architecture's rational lines, geometric patterns, classical aura, and distorted grandeur seem lifted from Giorgio de Chirico's metaphysical paintings. "Benito always was a plagiarist," de Chirico joked. He and Il Duce had shared an apartment in Bologna, back when the future dictator still edited *Il Popolo d'Italia*.

Il Duce was a showman, not a surrealist. His entire regime was a set for his ego. A gigantic relief of his bald head, set against a background of stylized *Sis*, adorned the façade of Palazzo Braschi, then the headquarters of the National Fascist Party, overlooking the Corso Vittorio Emanuele. Some public works had genuine substance, such as the town of Littorio in the Latina province, but most were *trompe l'oeil*. This was painfully obvious during Adolf Hitler's state visit in May 1938. Papier-mâché buildings were constructed, rivaling anything at

Cinecittà to make Rome appear more modern, wealthy, and powerful. The Führer was impressed, but not the Italian dialect poet, Trilussa, who wrote this famous epigram:

Roma de travertine,
Refatta de cartone
Saluta l'imbianchino,
Suo prossimo padrone.

Rome of travertine,
Remade with cardboard,
Greets the house painter
Who will be her next lord.

Of course, it ended in disaster. Mussolini tried to work men as other artists have worked marble or metals. But men are harder than stone and less malleable than iron. Ultimately, there was no masterpiece. All that remains of Il Duce's New Rome are botched fragments and tasteless monstrosities.

The Roma Termini train station, situated directly opposite the Baths of Diocletian, bears traces of Mussolini's original construction. The oppressively curved roof seems designed to remind commuters of imprisonment or deportation. The Foro Italico, Mussolini's grandiose sports complex at the foot of Monte Mario, still holds athletic events. Its naked, musclebound naked colossi grimace and brace for some terrible ordeal. Five miles south of Rome, however, is Mussolini's most ambitious project: the Esposizione Universale di Roma (EUR). Built for the aborted 1942 Olympics, this 420-acre business center and suburban complex was meant to showcase the glories of imperial Rome, past and present.

EUR's broad avenues, vast squares, and semicircular plazas are supposed to contrast with the clogged streets and narrow alleys of Rome's historic core. The park's most significant buildings stand at opposite ends of axial boulevards nearly a mile long. The most impressive and disturbing is the Palazzo della Civiltà Italiana, the Palace of Italian Civilization, better known as the Colosseo Quadrato (Square Coliseum). Like its namesake, this 160-foot office building consists of a series of superimposed loggias: six rows of nine arches each. These are the same number of letters, respectively, in Il Duce's first and last names.

The building's inscription is dedicated to "A PEOPLE OF POETS, ARTISTS, HEROES, SAINTS, THINKERS, SCIENTISTS, NAVIGATORS, AND VOYAGERS." The building's statuary is no less grandiose. Each corner of its podium features equestrian sculptures of Castor and Pollux, deliberately larger than the Cordonata Dioscuri in the Campidoglio. About the building's base are twenty-eight allegorical figures, approximately twelve feet high, each under an arch, representing various industries and trades. The building's interior, in fact, has been renovated to house the headquarters of Fendi, the luxury fashion company, which will pay 2.8 million euros a year to inhabit this Fascist EPCOT Center. The ground floor will contain exhibitions celebrating Italian craftsmanship.

Part theme park, part necropolis, EUR is both a frightening historical symbol and a popular film location. Here director Julie Taymor shot her nightmarish adaptation of Shakespeare's *Titus Andronicus*. At dusk, however, the complex eerily resembles Giorgio de Chirico's *Piazza d'Italia*. "The nostalgia of the infinite is revealed beneath the geometric precision of city squares," de Chirico said. Even the most Euclidean structures, however, eventually warp and crumble against time. Infinity is only an aspiration. The best art accepts transience and creates afflicted tributes to our fleeting humanity. The worst politics rejects the ephemeral and fossilizes every square inch of civilization.

Deborah Walker, author of *Giorgio de Chirico and the Real* (2008), argues that de Chirico's "mythologized streetscapes" depict an evolving space that is "no longer and not yet," much like Europe in the first decades of the twentieth century. The long nineteenth-century peace teetered on the brink of revolution, but no one could predict what total destruction was coming. A century later, we are poised at a similar turning point. As the sun sets on the EUR, we fear that tomorrow will annihilate today. In the dying light, the empty square confronts us with the inevitable move toward the strange and forbidding. Although the Colosseo Quadrato stands immutable, lengthening shadows suggest that our civilization already has passed away. The full reconciliation between our past and future, between internal torment and external stillness, remains incomplete. Until then, as darkness consumes the deserted city, de Chirico's ghost reminds us that humanity has left but has yet to arrive.

IX

Childhood and Its Derivatives

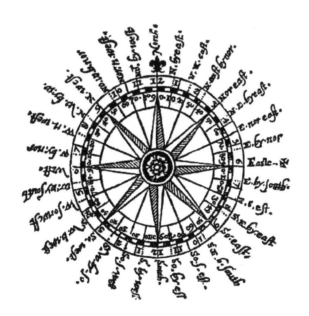

Andrei

The Eternal Children

THANKS TO ADVANCES IN MASS TRANSPORTATION, more people are crossing borders than ever before. More people claim multiple homelands than ever before. And, paradoxically, more people feel homeless than ever before. This alienation, however, isn't always a numb limbo in No Man's Land. Sometimes it is an agonizing trip to Neverland.

Meet the Lost Boys of the new millennium. Many immigrants, particularly exiles, leave as children, or with children in tow. Such early migration creates a terrible sense of detachment: from country, from culture and tradition, and, by extension, from a fragile self in the process of forming an identity. Not surprisingly, then, many immigrants remain in a state of perpetual childhood, regardless of how old they might be now, since this early phase of their life is frozen in time and cannot be revisited except on its own terms. The mind returns to the childhood scene of separation since this is the only way to make sense of its trauma. The primal wound becomes an eye to see, an ear to hear, a mouth to speak.

This process has created an unprecedented phenomenon on a global scale: *a generation of eternal children taking tentative root across six continents*. They see themselves and their past from a skewed vantage point, a slight remove. Consequently, they experience their native history and culture like foreigners. This explains why we have lost faith in national identity.

☾

Salman Rushdie, whose work often explores border crossing, cultural exchange, transience, and exile, speaks of "in betweenness." When one place is left behind, the possibility of going back somehow remains. As

Rushdie hints in an aptly titled essay, "A Dream of Glorious Return," for exiles such as himself, the dream of return never really fades, but lingers as a constant reminder of one's origins:

> I have left India many times. The first time was when I was thirteen and a half and went to boarding school in Rugby, England.... Since then my characters have frequently flown west from India, but in novel after novel their author's imagination has returned to it. This, perhaps, is what it means to love a country: that its shape is also yours, the shape of the way you think and feel and dream. That you can never really leave.

Andre Aciman—born in Egypt to French-speaking parents, who also were fluent in Italian, Greek, Ladino, and Arabic—would agree. His ancestors were Jews of Turkish and Italian origin who settled in Alexandria in 1905. Although he moved with his family to Italy at the age of fifteen and then to New York at nineteen, Aciman remains connected to his birthplace, which he sometimes revisits. "This marooned and spectral city," he explains in *False Papers: Essays on Memory and Exile*, "which is no longer home for me... would eventually find newer, ever more beguiling ways to remind me that here is where my mind always turns." Realizing that he always will end up in Alexandria ("even if I never come back") Aciman quotes his native city's most famous poet, Constantine Cavafy:

> For you won't find a new country.
>
> Won't find a new shore,
>
> The city will always pursue you,
>
> And no ship will ever take you away from yourself.

Rushdie uses the term "Imagi/Nation" to define *countries of the mind*, imaginary places to which we can hypothetically return at any moment as long as we turn our gaze inward and "dream ourselves" there. From the desert of alienation, we return to a land of milk and honey. "Exile," Rushdie says *The Satanic Verses*, "is a dream of glorious return." Unfortunately, the dream always fades. The imagined return stops feeling glorious. The dreamer awakes. The disappointment is galling. "I almost gave up on India," Rushdie admits, "almost believed the love affair was over for good."

Such is the case for many exiles. For some, the dream materializes and plays out like a fairy tale; for others, it remains unreachable—a mocking mirage at the horizon's edge.

☾

I have spent more than twenty years pursuing this dream, unsure if I've gotten any closer. In 2005, I took the first trip back to my native Romania after leaving the country with my parents in 1991. I spent two weeks visiting family, reliving old haunts, and traveling to popular destinations. Although born there, I was for all intents and purposes nothing more than a tourist. I returned once again for another two weeks in 2008 to present an academic paper at the University of Bucharest (on the topic of diaspora, of all things). Once again, I saw relatives, visited landmarks vaguely from childhood, and ventured to a few places I hadn't seen before.

I certainly plan to visit again but doubt the itinerary will change. By now, my homecoming has become routine and predictable, a "rite" of return. I enact a play in whose script I've been written and in which I have not only the inherited right to act but which I can't refuse to perform. Its pull reaches out across time and distance to wherever I might find myself. I practice this rite of return almost involuntarily, as if I am compelled to repeat the past in order to preserve it.

But what exactly am I preserving? At first I thought the answer was clear. I wanted to go back so I could reconnect with the extended family we had left behind in 1991: my ancestors, my heritage, the "real" me in my "true home." Everything, it seemed, was there. Everything had been left behind and only by returning would I be able to reclaim all that I had lost. Once back on Romanian soil, however, I realized how limited my childhood experiences had been. They were largely confined to our two-bedroom apartment in Bucharest's Third Sector, a working-class enclave: a park at the center of the city, where I remember playing among the branches of a low, crooked tree; my grandparents' farm in the country; and a few streets that loosely resembled those I'd left behind.

However, after revisiting these landmarks—once, twice—I was at a loss at what else to do next and felt little desire to see more. The country seemed a lot dirtier, crowded, and harder to navigate than I'd remembered when I was ten years old. I felt out of place in my own "home." And yet for more than fourteen years all I had dreamed of doing someday was returning back to this home. To this day the idea of going back still haunts me; it is a constant presence in my thoughts, as if only by returning can I become complete. It is a vicious cycle over which I seem to have no control.

Only recently have I come to understand my desire to return in different terms. This condition of heightened awareness, I realize, is only temporary and can change at any moment in the ever-shifting world of an exile's identity. I don't want to return to Romania per se, not the country of roughly twenty million people, of Transylvanian, Dracula-saturated lore, rapidly changing urban landscapes and sprawling multimillion dollar mansions. That is not *my* country. The Romania I want to visit is a country of nostalgia; a country suspended in childhood innocence; a country that exists only in my imagination: a Romania of the mind. Eva Hoffman's essay "The New Nomads" perfectly captures this process. "The lost homeland," she explains, "becomes sequestered in the imagination as a mythic, static realm." Like a wounded tree, the mind secretes resin and traps and preserves delicate winged memories in amber.

❧

Why, then, when I know that my country no longer exists, and likely never did, do I still want to return? Why does a nagging feeling always lurk in the back of all of my thoughts and through which I filter all of my present experiences? Is it possible for someone like myself to ever return? Do I even have the right to go back to a place I left so long ago? Do I have a choice in the matter or am I simply a participant in a ritual that I enact voluntarily or otherwise?

I have no answers. Exiles rarely do. Like Yukel, the eternal wanderer in Edmond Jàbes's *Book of Questions*, we are ill at ease with ourselves, "never *here*, always *elsewhere*," ahead of ourselves or behind like winter in the eyes of autumn or summer in the eyes of spring, in the past or in the future "like those syllables whose passages from night to day is so much like the lightning that it merges with the movement of the pen."

One Continuous

We did not live close to the sea, so we spent our afternoons shirtless with an axe in hand. We rode our dreams to and from the edge and came back with stories of the same news that flew in with the dust and the rain. The rain fell down—it tumbled without grace, without even a sign of dignity—in large chunks that left marks on our bare skin and tore through the crops to the center where we stood, to where someone was making love getting the morning cup ready rolling up soiled sleeves waiting for dawn in spite of what is known.

How little understanding we possessed back then. When one of us found a black egg on the ground—it was almost spring—he picked it up and held it to his ear like a shell. He cupped his hands and brought it even closer, told the rest of us to be silent. Because it did not speak he tossed it to the side and none of us looked where it fell. None of us could spare his infancy, not over an egg. None of us knew that we could do that. So we laughed instead, amused ourselves into stupid courage and marched ahead through the mud of childhood.

We were soiled and ragged—the children of opportunity, that's who— but we were not dangerous. Our games resembled the playful bite of a mongrel dog roaming the lamp-yellow streets without kin or master. The good moments fit on one hand with enough room to spare. And even those attributed to generosities of fate. . . . Or to the rain.

Oh, how we loved the rain. When it touched the embers with a hiss someone said, *Shhh . . . Listen.* And we all laughed some more at how absurd it sounded—the sheer possibility of it—staring down into the last good fire of the night, all of us aware of something endless and lonely, unnamable, something found on the side of the road, nearly erased, the color of all that we do not know—but there it is, there it is, like a voice in the distance.

What You Leave Behind

What you leave behind is a dandelion wish. Weathered by the wind. A stubborn weed in the middle of a field turned overnight metropolis.

What you leave behind are the stations of the sick. Sour breath everywhere and transparent, in your hair, in your teeth, in the blue-green filaments of your eyes. Hurry, hurry past the stations of the sick.

What you leave behind is your only love. Sonata on the lake at midnight lapping up the warm black water, the obsidian moon water, cool as silk in your hands. Running like a loose coin through your open hands.

What you leave behind are the windows with their long knitted curtains. The sunlight strained like flour, like water, like milk into the room. A maze of light, a web of blue light. Stay here a while, get lost inside this labyrinth a while.

What you leave behind is not a perversion of memory. A warped reflection twisting like a madman trapped inside a common stereotype. It is not nostalgia. It is not a love song to imagination. It is not religion.

What you leave behind are the many thin beds covered with the same brown-checkered wool. A universal blanket. Your own childhood blanket. Worn to the count of each single thread.

What you leave behind are versions, symbols, pieces holding each other's hands, theories, impulses, motives, the split of one inside two and two into four, numbered thoughts, a flash of lightning like a bridge in the distance.

What you leave behind are gray headlines, foreign news that make your shake your head in disbelief, in shame. The pictures are enough to tell a story.

What you leave behind are the vapid hours, long hours of watching traffic unfold like the map of a life you're still trying to understand. A street map that changes faster than it could be printed. Obsolete the day it is born.

What you leave behind is a nightlife that passes you by. Taxis idling in stereo at 3 a.m. out on the intersections.

What you leave behind is the smell of linden in the park. The heavy perfume on the escalators, on the marble stairs, in the elevator, the trail of it wrapped around the long white necks, the ankles, the curls about the waist.

What you leave behind is a Coke bottle of wine. Homemade wine, sour wine you pass around the table as the night fails at its promise and the insects are biting and it's too hot to sleep.

What you leave behind are those who knew you *when*, who could recognize your face. The Roman nose, barbarian eyes. You pitiful, unhappy clown.

What you leave behind is this black bag you drag with you everywhere. These shoes that have known too many miles. The aching bones of your feet.

What you leave behind is the bitch and her still blind litter on the esplanade. The homeless woman who made room for them on the square of cardboard she calls home. Leave your coin in your pocket for later and hurry, hurry, but you can't this time.

The Other Side Of

Among the destitute and the crippled where the streets were of dust and the sweeping was endless. An ordinary place to watch people come and go. No one said anything but the argument was the same from one eye to another. Subtle as scraping mold off bread in the morning before going to work with a bag in your hand and too many words in the mouth.

Lack thereof became a state of mind, almost transcendental. Knowledge beyond understanding. A whole kingdom of bullshit artists who know all there is to know and don't give a damn if they are told otherwise. They have yellowed collars to prove it. The blunt, dirty nails. At the dinner table they do not think twice about spit-shining a spoon. Sweet little nothings in a bigger scheme erased by the night.

I realize now that school cannot teach you that, church cannot teach you that; we practiced a junkyard religion. Got down in front of an altar of dirt and prayed with the wrong words because being right never made a saint of anyone. It never changed how things appear in daylight. Beautifully out of tune, improvised. Come quietly so you can hear it. Listen long and hard because it is deeper than us; it is deeper than all of us.

Antonio

Giovinezza (Pt. 1)

ON FEBRUARY 15, 1871, on leave from the University of Basel, Friedrich Nietzsche shared a coach to Lugano with Giuseppe Mazzini, who had returned from London to supervise the launch of his newspaper *La Roma del Popolo* in Pisa. Nietzsche, who idolized Mazzini, noticed that the old revolutionary spoke Italian with an English accent. Even his manners and dress were English. He traveled incognito as "George Brown, British gentleman" and wore a black Ulster coat. Wrapped in a tartan blanket, to protect his gaunt frame from the chill of the Italian Swiss Alps, Mazzini confided that he had been abroad for so long that he considered Italy a foreign country, and a depressing and disappointing one at that.

The journey through the Gotthard Pass proved dangerous. The narrow, winding road skirted one icy precipice after another. Near the Devil's Bridge, another coach failed to negotiate a hairpin turn, skidded, and fell into a chasm. To recover from the shock, the two men discussed German and Italian literature for the rest of the trip. Before they parted, Mazzini sighed. "Let us stay here in the land of fiction," he said, "for fictions are what give language to life. Not truth, not reality." Then Mazzini's sunken eyes blazed. Quoting Goethe, he told the young classics professor to live a life without compromise and to always risk everything. These words profoundly affected Nietzsche, who soon resigned his academic post at Basel to dedicate himself to writing.

Mazzini, the Apostle of the Risorgimento and the prophet of Western nationalism, had the same impact on an entire generation. He cultivated disaffection and idealism among the young and made them yearn and fight for a transfigured world. Nietzsche considered him a Superman. If Nietzsche was a philosopher who wanted to turn philosophy into poetry, Mazzini was a nationalist who wanted to turn his nation into a poem.

Born in 1805 into a middle-class Genoese family, Mazzini was a sickly but coddled child. He adored his father and mother, an anatomy professor and a devout Jansenist, whose advanced ideas and hothouse emotions shaped his thought and character. As an adult, Mazzini would try to recapture in causes and movements the intense familial love of his childhood. At first, the boy dreamed of becoming a historical novelist like Sir Walter Scott, whose poetry he recited. *Breathes there the man with soul so dead, who never to himself hath said, "This is my own, my native land!"* After giving alms to a fugitive rebel, however, Mazzini turned to politics. At fifteen, he began wearing black to mourn his oppressed homeland but remained almost willfully ignorant of the rest of Italy. He had traveled no farther than Tuscany before going into early and endless exile. He knew nothing of the Italian peasant masses and even less of its aristocracy. In spite of this, or because of this, he channeled and expressed the spirit of his time.

The Romantic era, a period of music and poetry, free love and revolution, was Western history's first mass youth movement. *"Bliss was it in that dawn to be alive,"* William Wordsworth declaims in his ode to the French Revolution, *"but to be young was very heaven."* Because of its rhapsodic quality, Milan Kundera calls this epoch the Lyrical Age. "Lyricism is intoxication," Kundera explains, "and man drinks in order to merge more easily with the world. Revolution has no desire to be examined or analyzed, it only desires that the people merge with it; in this sense it is lyrical and in need of lyricism."

To Italian youth, alienated by the philistinism of a mercantile society, oppressed by the brutality following the Congress of Vienna, Giuseppe Mazzini sang a hymn of mystical nationalism and universal brotherhood. Nations, he claimed, were not defined by such cold abstractions as law and commerce. They were animated and united by language and customs, historical tradition, and geographical continuity. Above all, by a common goal and a shared hope.

God, he believed, had given each country a sacred mission. Italy, because of its unique political and spiritual heritage, was destined to create a league of nations. The historical pattern was clear: "As the *Rome of the Caesars*, which unified much of Europe by Action, gave way to the *Rome of the Popes*, which by Thought unified Europe and America, so will the *Rome of the People* replace the other two, to unify the Faith of Thought and Action, Europe, America, and the rest of the terrestrial world."

To propagate this creed, Mazzini in 1831 founded *Giovine Italia* (Young Italy). This secret society was less a political movement than a religious cult. Like Peter the Hermit, Mazzini called for a crusade to liberate the Holy Land. His young disciples distributed tracts and preached the gospel of republican nationalism. Except for college students, few Italians were interested. Peasants felt loyalty only for their families, villages, and regions. Shopkeepers appreciated the efficiency of Italy's foreign rulers and asked only for lighter taxes. Aristocrats amused themselves within their private enclaves. If Mazzini had not been expelled, Young Italy would have died out in five years. Instead, it became a model for the young nationalist groups of the late-nineteenth and early-twentieth century: *Junges Deutschland, Młoda Polska, Genç Türkler.*

From London, Mazzini wrote articles, raised money, and recruited followers for the Italian revolution. English intellectuals and politicians, such as Thomas Carlyle, Charles Dickens, George Eliot, and William Gladstone, hailed him a statesman. Italian authorities and even some of his fellow nationalists, such as Cavour and Gioberti, denounced him as a terrorist: a sallow-faced fanatic who brooked no opposition and had no compunction about manipulating and sacrificing the impressionable and the naive. "The Apostle," said novelist and historian Robert Katz, "sent more young idealists to glorious but meaningless death than perhaps any other man in history save Stalin—wrenching his pure heart and soul." Francesco Bentivegna, Attilio and Emilio Bandiera, and Carlo Piscane died horribly, sometimes at the hands of the very peasants they had fought to free, for a cause that had proven obscene.

While exiled in England, Mazzini was spared this disillusionment. He loved London more than his native Genoa. Its fog suited his melancholy disposition. Its matrons appreciated his chaste flirting and sighed at his soulful guitar playing. Its tobacconists supplied him with cheap cigars. Living among strangers, losing his mother tongue but starting an Italian school for immigrants, Mazzini could love only an imaginary homeland. When he returned and discovered that United Italy was nothing but a cheap imitation of the United Kingdom, a free-trading, self-loving, smooth-running, liberal, imperialist, nation-state-machine, not the Third Rome envisioned by Dante, Petrarch, and Machiavelli, he felt betrayed. "I thought I had awakened the soul of Italy," he lamented, "and all I can see is her corpse." When he died of pleurisy in 1872, he was still a fugitive. Arrested and imprisoned in Gaeta for planning an insurrection in Sicily, Mazzini had been released but never pardoned. For the next fifty years, few monuments commemorated him.

"A prophet is not without honor," Jesus had said, "except in his native land." Abroad, Mazzini continued to inspire such diverse figures as Jane Addams, Mahatma Gandhi, Leo Tolstoy, Woodrow Wilson, and Sun Yat-sen, dreamers and visionaries who sought to convert the young. At home, despite perfunctory textbook eulogies, Mazzini was an embarrassing anachronism. Politicians detested his radicalism. Prelates condemned his religion of God and the People. Businessmen resented his antimaterialism. Socialists scoffed at his nationalism. Except for immigrants at Hull House, who pined for an imaginary Italy amid the offal of the Chicago stockyards, nobody read *The Duties of Man*. But one young agitator in Bologna shared the Apostle's dream of a Third Rome. His name was Benito Mussolini.

Andrei

Psalm for the Children of the Rain

The water gathers in ruts down the middle of a one-way street. There are children ankle deep in the mud deciding on the new rules of the game. In the kitchen God hangs in balance between a chipped pot and the carved wooden ladle. Grandmother uses the unknown to explain the unknown and everything has an answer, which goes without saying. When she falls asleep she lays across her chest the heavy book of her hand.

The children are still out there playing. They are a sentence that ends in a question mark whose answer makes for good food and good politics. Feet in the mud, water covered, clouded. The good light that is never planned. It falls on the perfect nose and the sky colored eye on an ordinary day in the city of your dreams. It goes unnoticed and sleeps beneath a curb with the vagabonds and the shimmer of stars. Childhood love, where did you go when I wasn't looking? It's been years, it's been a whole life of befores and afters, a gallery of pictures on the walls of the loveless.

Our small obsessions wear us down into sand where before there was nothing but stone. Into almost nothing at all. We become scattered, we become notes tacked to a wall, boxes of love letters gone yellow and musty unanswered in a basement cupboard. Next to the spoons, the hand-me-down dishes. The book of my grandmother's hand is full of such stories, of mud and blood and of women who were no good by the color scheme of their bedrooms and from the way they held a child in their arms. God has forgotten about them, she would say. God has forgotten about the children getting dirty. Teach them to stay out of the water, teach them to come in when the road is too deep to cross.

The Plot Against

Wood creaks and a child thinks about vestigial roads that wind beneath the white ribs of the night. She keeps the customary silence of a seed that falls just to remember the way up again. In the blindness of fog she uses what she knows—the smell of dirt, manure, damp earth, fruit left too long in the orchard. *Have you ever plucked a sour grape from its tendril, felt the mouth go dry, taste buds taking refuge? Remember how your face twisted even as you smiled?* A child's childhood—each year the same, seeds yet to inhabit their sweetness—in the air hints of apple, touch of dust after a summer rain. She closes her eyes and feels the mud on her boots, the grass trampled underfoot, the need to keep moving.

Vignette

Those were hungry years when anything was possible. We hitched them on our backs and carried the days around like beaded necklaces, beautiful burdens we were too young to untangle.

From a bricked-in circle fires inched upward to the edge of fingertips kneading the cold. Small fires for the young, branches and grass to burn what they didn't yet know could be burned. Logs and coal to keep a slim light going through the night.

There were pots and pans in the sink that we scrubbed getting ready for company. We scrubbed them every day—we wanted to give off an impression. Children scrubbed behind their ears with cold water and lye. Some things are never clean enough.

Anyone could see this was true if they bothered to look around. But the eyes were used to looking down, counting our toes. Something kept our heads down, told us to count one more time for the answer, but we never did get it right.

Antonio

Giovinezza (Pt. 2)

"WE ARE WORKING TO TRANSLATE INTO FACT the aspirations of Giuseppe Mazzini," wrote Benito Mussolini in the December 7, 1921, issue of *Il Popolo d'Italia*: "to give the Italians a 'religious concept of their nation.'" Four months later, after the March on Rome gave Mussolini absolute power, the dictator declared himself Mazzini's "truest disciple." Italian liberals balked, but the philosopher Giovanni Gentile, the new Minister of Education, made Il Duce's case.

Mazzini, Gentile claimed, had *never* favored the kind of effete democratic nationalism, based simply on self-determination, which that schoolmaster Woodrow Wilson had advocated in Paris. On the contrary, Mazzini's thought was hostile to bourgeois liberalism and rooted in a profoundly spiritual vision of life. For Mazzini, rights derived from *duties*, and a nation could only claim rights when its citizens had demonstrated a capacity to struggle in pursuit of a shared ethical goal. Nations were spiritual entities, and freedom consisted of the individual immersing his moral being in that of the whole. Fascism would instill these values in Italy's youth, which was why the Party had adapted as its anthem "*Giovinezza*," a popular trench song:

> *Giovinezza, giovinezza*
> *Primavera di bellezza!* . . .

> Youth, youth, spring of beauty!
> Amid life's hardship, your song rings and goes!

To turn children into Fascists, Mussolini created the *Opera Nazionale Balilla* (ONB), a national youth organization. This scouting and paramilitary group honored Giuseppe Mazzini's childhood hero

Balilla (Little Squirt), a ten-year-old Genoese boy whose real name was Giovan Battista Perasso. An early symbol of the Risorgimento, Balilla had started the revolt of 1746 against the Hapsburg forces occupying Genoa in the War of the Austrian Succession. As artillerymen dragged a mortar along a muddy road in the Portoria district, the gun got stuck in a moat. The soldiers forced onlookers to dislodge it, cursing and lashing them. Outraged, Ballila grabbed a stone from the road and asked the crowd: "*Che l'inse?*" ("Shall I start?") The boy flung the stone, hit an officer in the forehead, and sparked a riot that drove the garrison from Genoa.

The ONB was divided into different groups, according to age and gender: *Figli della Lupa* (Children of the She-Wolf, an allusion to Romulus and Remus): boys and girls, ages 6 to 8; *Balilla* (boys) and *Piccole Italiane* (girls): ages 8 to 14; *Avanguardisti* (boys) and *Giovani Italiane* (girls): ages 14 to 18. The government supervised all school activities and pressured teachers to enlist all students. Besides "Fascist Saturdays," children would spend their summers at Campo Dux, a state camp. Boys wore a uniform consisting of a black shirt; a fez borrowed from the *Arditi,* the storm troopers of World War I; khaki trousers; black fasces emblems; and a blue neckerchief. During military exercises, they drilled with a *Moschetto Balilla,* a scaled-down version of Royal Italian Army service rifle, and sang the *Balilla* hymn: "*Fischia il sasso! Il nome squilla!*" The stone whistles! Trumpet the name of the boy from Portoria! Intrepid Ballila, he is a giant in history!

"Fascism won," bragged Asvero Grevelli, a party hack who was rumored to be Il Duce's bastard, "because it had better songs." History supports this claim. Most Italian boys eagerly joined the chorus of "*Duce a Noi*" and "*Inno dei Figli della Lupa.*" During the invasion of Ethiopia, they switched to "*Faccetta Nera*" ("Little Black Face'), serenading an Abyssinian girl with promises of freedom, until Mussolini banned the song for supposedly encouraging miscegenation. Fathers were proud when their grown sons enrolled in the *Squadracce,* squads of black-shirted men who sang popular Fascist hymns and hammered them into people's heads, quite literally.

American historians smile at this spectacle. Only a nation addicted to opera and corrupted by Gabriele D'Annunzio's bombastic verse could be overthrown by totalitarian lyricism. But young people everywhere are susceptible to bad music and bad poetry. "This vulnerability expresses the basic situation of immaturity," Milan Kundera explains in *Life is Elsewhere*; "lyricism is an attempt to face that situation." Expelled from the protected enclosure of childhood, teenagers wish to enter the world; but at the same time, because the world frightens them, they fashion "an artificial replacement world" out of music and lyrics. These songs and poems revolve around them "like the planets around the sun." Encased in an armillary sphere, the naive become "the center of a small universe in which nothing is alien," in which they feel "as much at home as a child inside its mother, for everything here is fashioned only from the substance of [their] soul." Every playlist and canon expresses a desire to return to the womb.

What is true of iPods and the Norton anthology is true of politics. National myths are both preprogrammed siren songs and officially sanctioned poems. Nowhere is this truer than in the United States, perhaps the only Western country that takes it national anthem seriously and asks citizens to pledge allegiance to its flag. America still believes in providential history, still insists on its exceptionalism, still proclaims itself a light unto the nations. Now Italian historians smile, for this national faith comes not only from the Puritans and the Founders, who called the United States a City on a Hill and the New Order of the Ages, but also from Giuseppe Mazzini: the Apostle of United Italy and the Father of the European Union. The Young American Movement, founded in 1845, was modeled after Young Italy. John L. O'Sullivan, its most eloquent spokesperson, was a Mazzinian as much as a Jeffersonian. A believer in Romantic nationalism, he coined the term Manifest Destiny to describe America's unique role in world events. O'Sullivan never meant to justify genocide, imperialism, and militarism, but then Mazzini never imagined validating Mussolini.

Will humanity ever live in a postnational world, free from the illusions of God and country? This is Salman Rushdie's central question in *Imaginary Homelands*. National myths presume to give us meaning and identity by presenting us with a total picture. "But human beings," Rushdie points out, "do not perceive things whole; we are not gods but wounded creatures, cracked lenses, capable only of fractured perceptions. Partial beings, in all the senses of that phrase. Meaning is a shaky edifice we build out of scraps, dogmas, childhood injuries, newspaper articles, chance remarks, old films, small victories, people hated, people loved; perhaps it is because our sense of what is the case is constructed from such inadequate materials that we defend it so fiercely, even to the death."

Fortunately, migrants and immigrants can step out of nationalism's vicious hermeneutical circle and achieve a cosmopolitan freedom—provided they don't succumb to nostalgia or fanaticism. More often, unfortunately, they suffer from arrested development in ethnic ghettos or betray everything around them and mindlessly assimilate, merely swapping one myth for another. Unable to imagine themselves as either yuppies or jihadists, Dzhokhar and Tamerlan Tsarnaev exploded two bombs at the Boston Marathon on Patriots' Day, partly to protest America's ongoing wars in Afghanistan and Iran but also to support independence for Chechnya, a country they claimed as their homeland but had never visited except on the Web. This madness will continue, Milan Kundera says, as long as we believe that "life is elsewhere." When will we accept that it is here and now?

X

Here and Now

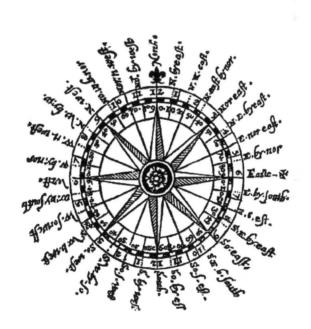

Andrei

Make Beautiful, Again

"AWAKEN, ROMANIAN, FROM YOUR SLEEP OF DEATH!" So exhorts the national anthem *Deşteaptă-te, române*, which the great nationalist Nicolae Bălcescu called "the Romanian *Marseillaise*." Composed for the Wallachian Revolution of 1848, this anthem marked the worst Romanian bloodbaths of the twentieth century. It was sung on December 15, 1917, when the Moldavian Democratic Republic was established. It was sung on August 23, 1944, when Romania turned against Nazi Germany. It was sung on December 30, 1947, when the Romanian Communist Party came to power. It was sung on Christmas Day, 1989, when the Ceauşescus were summarily executed.

For this reason, *Deşteaptă-te, române* evokes mixed feelings. On the one hand, the anthem's stirring lyrics have inspired hope and courage: "*Acum ori niciodată croieşte-ţi altă soarte!*" Now or never create a new fate for yourself! On the other hand, the anthem's fantasies of revenge and glory—its promise to make powerful enemies bow in supplication, its boast in the blood of Trajan running through Romanian veins, its invocation of such "imperial shadows" as Michael the Brave, Stefan the Great, and Matthias the Just—have brought Romania repeatedly to the brink of annihilation. How many times and in how many ways must we be urged to shake off the dust of the past and march into the future?

𝄞

Romania's dilemma is universal. Ultimately, humanity's own fear, hatred, and resentment keep it trapped in illusions. Yet from these illusions spring culture and language, the things that make us most human. Unable to live in the present, we pine for a lost Eden in the past or imagine a New Jerusalem in the future. That's why we are so easily duped and enslaved by religious and political myths—and are driven to murder, war, and genocide to either achieve these goals or to express our inevitable disappointment. "When we kill great dreams," Milan Kundera says in *Life is Elsewhere*, "much blood is shed."

How do we break this vicious cycle of despair, bad faith, and atrocity? Do we abandon history? Not likely. History will not abandon us. The past always rebukes the present. Do we escape into poetry then? Such escapism leads straight to hell. Ezra Pound tried to save Western civilization by writing the *Cantos*. "Make It New!" he had urged his generation, convinced that poetry could resurrect the past, redeem the present, and secure the future. Instead, he became a rabid anti-Semite and a fascist propagandist and was confined in an insane asylum. If we don't want to repeat the political and artistic mistakes of the twentieth century, what should we do?

We might begin by rejecting the idea that human beings are special; give up all forms of salvation and immortality, both religious and secular; and embrace our own impermanence. Rather than make the world forever new, we should be content to make it temporarily bearable. Rather than seek control, we should relinquish it. The only order—in life or art—is chaos. New York City's beauty, Franz tells Sabina in *The Unbearable Lightness of Being*, is "unintentional." "It arose," he explains, "independent of human design, like a stalagmitic cavern. Forms which are in themselves quite ugly turn up fortuitously, without design, in such incredible surroundings that they sparkle with a sudden wondrous poetry."

But what if there was a way to bring a kind of order to that chaos, to simultaneously embrace design and fortuity? Marcel Duchamp claimed to have been the first artist to embrace and make use of chance occurrence in his artwork. Clearly he was also prone to moments of aggrandizing. In a famous episode he is said to have flipped a coin in order to decide whether to remain in Paris of leave for New York. He flipped the coin and had to leave for New York. If Paris is where chance made its way onto the arts scene, then maybe New York is where it will be resuscitated.

I say resuscitated, though reimagined might also be appropriate. If we accept a common view of contemporary art that says innovation is no longer possible at the level of content (i.e., it's all been done before), then one must look instead at innovation in terms of form. While it may not be exactly *new*, it might be *new enough*, or at least not easily replicated.

☙

New York–based photographer Brent Alan Williamson creates many of his works using his own homemade black and white film, which he leaves "unpolished." The chemicals are applied to the film strip unevenly, almost haphazardly, creating rough spots and gaps in the finished product. He then proceeds to shoot entire rolls using this purposefully distressed film, never knowing what the results will be.

By giving in to process, entire shots and even film rolls might be ruined, with subjects blotted out or cut off by the placement of the film surface's random alignment. And sometimes, by sheer chance or accident, the subject in a certain frame will align with the contours within the film itself in such a way as to complement one another, to create an image that could not have been conceived through artistic vision alone. Williamson is ultimately driven by the principle that despite the full presence of the artist in the process, photography is a subconscious effort on the part of both photographer and model, becoming ultimately an act of liberation from the confines of convention. However, the resulting work in itself cannot be considered unconventional or unique solely at level of content. One might even call it typical, with titles such as "Nude Reclining on Chair," or "Figure Looking Out of the Window," easily ascribed to some of his pieces. The innovation occurs at the level of form or design. In his work, the altered medium meets common, traditional content, forcing the viewer into a new language required to engage with and make sense of the final product (not unlike a surrealist painting that conjures a more fluid and malleable language of the imagination).

To trigger the imagination, then, to have it fire in new directions, one must be open to the possibilities offered by the juxtaposition of the unexpected—random occurrence and the discerning, subjective and critical eye filtering every moment. In Williamson's case, the artist's effort represents a purposeful engagement, by way of design, with chance and randomness, yet one that endows the artist with a certain degree of control over the process—it is a marriage between complete chaos and the control that as human beings it is in our nature to seek out and which we cannot seem to escape—all of which might just suggest a way forward in a world increasingly defined by either minute technological control over process and product, or wholesale dismissal of the role of the creator. The result, when the dice or the film and subject fall just so, could very well be Kundera's cherished "unintentional beauty." In other words, "beauty by mistake."

☾

To embrace this kind of beauty, however, takes courage. It means embracing irredeemable loss, accepting that life might never happen quite the way we want it to. It means confronting a posthuman world and abandoning all fairy-tale prescriptions for living happily ever after. We must forget "happy" and "ever after" and simply live. "The certitude that there is no salvation is a form of salvation," said the Romanian philosopher E. M. Cioran; "in fact, it *is* salvation. Starting from here, we might organize our own life as well as construct a philosophy of history and art: the insoluble as solution, as the only way out."

Yet this might be the only way to make peace with our fate, to interrupt the cycle of bad faith—surrender ourselves to an impulse of creation, which maybe, just maybe, will keep us from destroying this planet in the name of freedom and progress. That has been poetry's forlorn hope since at least the Romantic era:

> Though nothing can bring back the hour
> Of splendor in the grass, of glory in the flower;

We will grieve not, rather find

Strength in what remains behind;

In the primal sympathy

Which having been must ever be...

—William Wordsworth, *Ode: Intimations of Immortality*

Building Blocks

People are fashioning time out of simple things again, out of the scent and out of the water, the drops filling a teacup left out on the curb, its miniature spoon still sweet from the tongue. This is how *know thyself* was conceived, through the steady addition of rain, the lull between waves. It was churned inside the mouth wrapped around olive oil and bread. The span it took for the dough to rise. A broken cloud becomes a clearing, a passing that can be understood as different from same, a light skimming the overflowed saucer, an after without name.

When Turning Toward

Children's watercolors left to curl along the wall, age enamored tossing as the heat fell down into the well of night and gained the function of a shiver. Any sense of what is good was guided by a rose bouquet and red enamel sky, the land sprawling heavyset in broad strokes at the bottom. Always the land. Beautifully violent. Its will and art meandering inside a labyrinth of culture bought and paid for. The clothes on your back bought and paid for, worthless for what they cannot hold. Your arms worthless for what they have forgotten. How heavy to lift the head each morning when you are born into the twists and turns of an alley given by name to the glory of tears. Born to inhabit a house of the unsaid and tears. Each one louder as the cold sets in, the cold that makes the paper stiffen as you pass from one room to the next, the body passing through the years in treason to itself—turning to the inward eye, gathering color, stroke by stroke, the world as it should be coming into view as it never was.

Make Beautiful

In the wee hours we conduct small acts of sabotage. It is a solitary joy. Learning how to watch the fall of things more insignificant than us. How to be their architect. It even has the look of revelation, of the artful rendering—without music, our two hands moving to the violent strokes etched in a tablature too worn and memorized—like some kind of truth—love that is all form without context—"Death's favorite photograph," someone says in recognition—a 4x6 a little on the wrinkled side and stuffed in a back pocket as he walks the empty halls, his white cane pecking its way. . .

℆

All before the blue dawn of birds balancing their weightlessness. And then the lined up silences accusatory—what have you done, what did not make it through the night? Half blind, we take inventory and nothing adds up—always too little or too much and the notes on the bedside table are illegible with sleep. Something you can't put a finger on takes the shape of a cloud—then another and another—until it is only blue again. In that mocking clarity of morning when you're alone at the kitchen table with a flame and the empty pan just starting to crackle, the cupboards all empty. . .

℆

Who knows the effort that it takes to get up and do it all over again? Continents shift imperceptibly in our lifetime. Entire continents! And their backs, too, cave in on themselves, grow smaller each year. Who can know? The note on the table says something about a carnival, lights on the water, possibly caught in the salty kiss of the sea. There should have been voices, I know this—but that last part is rubbed out with a fury I don't recall. Yet another thing that happens without sound inside a burst of color. And again the hour when the golden hills thrown to the distance hunker down to better hold the light. That's exactly what I used to draw once. Over and over until I had created an entire country. I felt brave enough to do that.

Antonio

Apollo Atones (Pt. 1)

"To write poetry after Auschwitz," Theodore Adorno declared, "is barbaric." What exactly did the German philosopher and sociologist mean by this statement? Adorno neither believed that poetry was dead nor wished to deny concentration camp survivors the right to bear witness through their words. But he did think that to continue writing poetry based on the same unexamined assumptions that had caused the Holocaust was cruel. Adorno rejected all artistic attempts to reconstruct the ruins of Western civilization. Any such attempt, he argued, citing Nietzsche, merely would construct a hollow stage set or, worse, would replicate totalitarianism.

Art is not salvation, Adorno insisted. Modernism, a continuation of Romanticism's rebellion against the industrial and scientific revolutions, had made a religion of art. But by trying to compensate for the death of God, art had committed or celebrated atrocity. The brazier from the Pythian shrine had consumed all Europe. The world was shocked when Apollo, the god of light, the patron of music and poetry, stood in the dock at Nuremberg; but Greek myth had long testified to his crimes. He flayed Marysas alive, for example, because the satyr had dared to challenge him to a music contest. Like a Nazi commandant, Apollo cut and tanned the hide and sewed Marysas into a wineskin. According to Diodorus Siculus, Apollo felt so guilty for what he had done that he put aside his lyre as a penance.

For a while, music and poetry disappeared from the earth. Inevitably, they returned. The Muses refused to let humanity perish from lack of beauty. But when Apollo began composing again, he did so in a different key. Atonement had retuned his lyre. We must do the same. Unless we confront and repent the cruelty of the past century, particularly cruelty perpetrated in the name of some bright, shining ideal, we will never rehabilitate beauty.

Ezra Pound, the godfather of Modernist poetry, wanted to renew Western culture and protect it from self-destruction. Bad writing, he believed, destroyed civilizations; good writing saved them. During World War I, Pound began the *Cantos*. Modeled after the great epics from Homer to Dante, this *magnum opus* was supposed to be a heroic harrowing of hell. Like a seer, Pound would guide readers through the cyclone of history to reach the calm eye of revelation. Unfortunately, the *Cantos* became a clearinghouse for Pound's increasingly toxic ideas about politics and economics. An international conspiracy of Jewish bankers, he maintained, had engineered and profited from the Great War. Anglo-American democracy was morally bankrupt. The acid test of a civilization was whether it fostered the arts. Pound's haphazard survey of history had convinced him that art flourished most in societies with a strong leader, a stable hierarchy, and an agrarian economy.

After the war, Pound moved to Italy and fell in love with Benito Mussolini, whom he met at a violin concert given by his mistress, Olga Rudge, at Villa Torlonia. Il Duce, he was convinced, was the reincarnation of Sigismondo Malatesta, the Wolf of Rimini, the sixteenth-century warlord, poet, and patron of the arts lionized in Cantos VIII to XI. Over the next six years, Pound courted the Italian dictator. He joined Filippo Tommaso Marinetti and other former Futurists, now card-carrying Fascists, and solicited state funding for the arts. He wrote mash notes in the press and published a pamphlet comparing Mussolini to Jefferson. Finally, Pound was granted a private audience at Palazzo Venezia, where he presented Il Duce with an autographed copy of *A Draft of XXX Cantos*. "*Ma questo è divertente*," Mussolini drawled. How *very* entertaining. From this ironic remark, Pound concluded that Mussolini had an intuitive grasp of his poetry's significance. He would become this philosopher-king's minister of culture.

When Italy entered World War II, Pound delivered a series of rabid radio broadcasts from Rome. He maligned the Jews, denounced

Franklin Roosevelt, and criticized American intervention. The broadcasts continued through the Allied invasion of Italy. While Mussolini was installed in the Republic of Salò, a Nazi puppet state near Lake Garda, Pound wrote two propagandistic cantos in Italian, praising Fascism's fighting spirit. After Germany surrendered Italy to the Allies on May 2, 1945, Pound was reported to the U.S. Army authorities. A federal grand jury had indicted the poet on thirteen counts of treason. Pound was formally arrested and brought to the U.S. Army Disciplinary Training Center north of Pisa, kept in an outdoor cage for two and a half weeks. After a physical breakdown, he was moved to a medical tent, where he typed poems on a rust-eaten Corona. On November 15, he was transferred to the United States, subjecting the escorting officer during the transatlantic flight to crackpot rants. Ten days later he was arraigned in D.C.

Through the intercession of powerful patrons, Pound was sent for psychiatric evaluation to St. Elizabeth's: then a federal mental hospital, now the headquarters of the Department of Homeland Security. For a time, he was held for observation at the prison ward, Howard Hall (better known as the Hellhole), locked in a padded room with a thick steel door and nine peepholes. While other patients wandered the hall, screaming and frothing at the mouth, psychiatrists studied Pound. They concluded that he suffered from paranoid schizophrenia and was unfit to stand trial.

Prosecutors rightly suspected the diagnosis. Declassified documents show that the doctors had exaggerated Pound's condition because he was such a fascinating specimen, not to mention a literary celebrity. But the public outrage was nothing compared to the national furor when Pound won the 1949 Bollingen Prize for the *Pisan Cantos*, which he had begun writing on toilet paper while caged in the army camp. Some poems seemed like genuine recantations ("Pull down thy vanity!"), but others read like unapologetic elegies for Fascism. Pound compared Mussolini—shot by partisans and hung by his heels from the girder of a Milanese gas station—to the crucified Christ. "Poetry," thundered the *Pittsburgh Post-Gazette*, "[cannot] convert words into maggots that eat at human dignity and still be good poetry."

Pound spent the next eight years in St. Elizabeth's, where he worked on the *Cantos* and sent cryptic postcards to friends. Prominent writers lobbied on his behalf. Ernest Hemingway, using his Nobel Prize as leverage, campaigned for his release. Archibald MacLeish, the former Librarian of Congress, asked the iconoclastic New Deal lawyer Thurman Arnold to file a *pro bono* petition to dismiss Pound's indictment. On April 14, 1958, the same judge who had committed Pound to the asylum ordered his release. The Department of Justice did not object. Pound returned to Italy in July. As he walked off the boat in Naples, the poet was mobbed by reporters, who asked him when he had been released from the madhouse. "I never was," Pound replied. "When I left the hospital I was still in America, and all America is an insane asylum." He cackled and gave the Fascist salute.

After such knowledge, what forgiveness?

Andrei

Approaching Stalemate

The first time I drew tomorrow I used too much color. The curtains in
the sun were beautifully helpless and the fruit on the table spoke with a
common voice. I put in there a common woman with the common tip
of a nose but the blue eyes were overdone, overgrown with the ruin of
that fleeting sentiment.

When reconstructing days you'll never see again it's easy to make such
a mistake. Nothing is bolted to the sky or to the earth and comes back
from an errant flight wearing a riddle's fine trimmings. It resembles
something you might love when the passing of summer makes for a
necessary performance. Next time, to be safe, better to stick to par-
ticulars, universal gray where a bird spat on the ground and stained its
shadow with a less-than-complicated metaphor. Everything becomes
reduced in time to simpler things—

for example, I enjoy Beethoven's minimal constellations and the occasional picnic followed by a leisurely walk home. The grass undulates
but the wind is not enough to bother the branches and so they go
unnoticed, ostracized from memory, though one could imagine, quite
literally, that the empty spot on the easel could be them. A surrogate
anniversary that's as a pretty as you want it to be.

If I had a palette unsuffered by the breach of color—and the discord between skill and appetite—I would have painted instead what the menu
suggested—an interim angel of between-black-and-white. Equinox
angel of space that has yet to become brocaded word—recognizable
chaos. Pinned to the sky she would look down like any other icon in

the kitchens of the already judged. And the breeze would come in off the early lake with all of the lust it could muster and the sweat would gather in the corner of the eye making it hard to see.

The Exact Reasons

I

A toast, to the brutal beauty of your flowering mouth, my brother, to the walking wounded dragging the rags of their soul through the mud and the age of linear events to the scattered tombs of our unmarked love. You resemble Dionysus lost among the glass futures, brilliant crystal of many faces. The suffering of your being is stretched like Christ across canvas without arms, without so much as an absence I can light a candle for, the yellow wax a figure in my palms.

II

Since you left I haven't left this garden. I think of ways of shoring up the fences, I sharpen the scythe and my anger angers the stone simply doing its job. Brother, your figure is a woman and a child and a man trembling from laughter, from the unlettered dove flying through its own ailing shadow over the wheat fields stalking the land. Into your wild eyes and into your thirst I will drown what's left of this day and of always and its secrets. I will walk under the chestnut trees and see part of sky, part of ground, part of a lily opening and dying like a fist, part of parts of myself.

III

Brother, a continent has shrunk down to the size of this room, this chair, this intimacy broken over the sacred cup. The night has rolled up its sleeves and it's getting ready for work. Remember when we were filled with the same blood? How much I miss you and your lust and your fears, your stomach roaring with guilt and that brief torment of happiness. A toast then, for what can be read in each hand on a street corner in the language and law of the coin—life, this hour and this life, its irrational waters murmuring like birds in love, like dumb birds that know without knowing.

Otherwise a Life

No, the end is not in our sights, it has been the farthest thing from the truth; this near-incessant humming of base need. Here, the body aches for what comes closest to now; touch me it says, I am present only under, beneath, weighed by and down.

How else to know something is lacking? My future self greets your future self and they are bored with old drinking tales—remember when? Of course, how could I not, you're always there to remind me when the perfume wears down to a breeze.

The end, we were talking about the end—woman, were you not the reason I swore to forget all of it, leave all of it, make it new, make other, make what hasn't been imagined by God? I am present by the aforementioned touch, by word, by whiskey-warm breath. I am the hum and the not-yet of nighttime betrayals. Morning will shed its skin to bare it bright and honest and we will close our eyes a little while longer.

At first light it begins to end some more; the last of it is on the bloody blade of a horizon, quaint and common, archetype of choose-your-own-impossible-to-dream. The odds are what they are; but we've a couple tricks left up our sleeves—wink wink *Yes* and *Yes* my dear—I will believe in games if you can pawn along with me until the edge of wood and field where we can trade each other for the queen of hearts. Pretend. Pretend. Make it a ritual. Otherwise a life.

Antonio

Apollo Atones (Pt. 2)

"WE COME AFTER," George Steiner says in *Language and Silence*. "We know now that a man can read Goethe or Rilke in the evening, that he can play Bach and Schubert, and go to his day's work at Auschwitz in the morning. To say that he has read them without understanding or that his ear is gross, is cant." How does this revelation bear on literature and society; on the faith proclaimed from Plato to Matthew Arnold that culture humanizes; on Keats's assertion that beauty is truth, truth beauty, and that is all we need to know on earth? Discovering that we are monsters, should we renounce beauty and punish ourselves forever? Should we put out our eyes because the light is unbearable? Should we pierce our eardrums and pull out our tongues?

Ezra Pound rarely spoke in exile. Silence was his penance and solace, a way of atoning for his wartime broadcasts, of mourning the death of such irreplaceable friends as H.D., T. S. Eliot, and William Carlos Williams, of confessing that his unfinished and unfinishable *Cantos* were a failure. He could not make the poem cohere. He had tried to reconstruct the great rose window of Dante's *Paradiso*, but the window had shattered and had sprayed him with shards of stained glass. He had lost his center fighting the world. His dreams had crashed. His errors and wrecks lay about him. He had gone to pieces. "You—find me—in fragments," he told Donald Hall in a 1960 interview for the *Partisan Review*.

The broken old man divided his time between Sant'Ambrogio, a villa in the hills above Rapallo, and the Bird's Nest, a townhouse in Venice on Calle Querini Dorsoduro, a cul-de-sac behind the Basilica of Santa Maria della Salute. Age made him look more than ever like a bard. His unruly hair and wild beard had turned white. His nose was a shrike's beak; his fingers were bones. During his November walks in Piazza San Marco, bundled against the wind and the rain, Pound would stroll through a whirlwind of pigeons. He wore a black coat, a wide-brimmed hat, a frayed scarf, and a tattered cape, "the dress of a pilgrim-seer," says biographer James Wilhelm, "making a journey toward some unknown land." Former friends, passing through Venice and catching a glimpse of him, compared him to King Lear.

Pound might have remained on the heath forever, if not for Allen Ginsberg. The Beat poet appeared one sunny June day in 1967 in the garden of Pound's villa, sitting cross-legged under a dogwood and playing Indian mantras on a hurdy-gurdy. Fresh from a pilgrimage to Mayapur, Kyoto, and Marrakesh, Ginsberg had written Pound in St. Elizabeth's, so Olga invited him to come inside. Ginsberg reeked of marijuana, but his effusiveness disarmed Pound, who listened as Ginsberg played LPs from his knapsack: Dylan, Donovan, the Beatles. Pound said nothing but tapped his cane to "Eleanor Rigby." When he heard the lyrics *No one was saved,* a smile flickered on his lips. Otherwise, his face remained expressionless, his body rigid. The old sphinx would not speak, however, until their next meeting.

On October 28, the two men lunched at Pensione Cici Restaurant, right around the corner from Pound's townhouse. Ginsberg, whose mother had been institutionalized for paranoid schizophrenia, confided that he had heard William Blake's voice in Harlem. Pound started, pursed his lips, and looked away. He, too, had heard voices. Not all of them had been angels. But it was more than hearing a voice, Ginsberg continued. For weeks, he had experienced an altered state of consciousness. Did that make sense? Pound nodded. *Yes, that makes sense. But my work makes no sense.* Ginsberg disagreed. Despite everything that had gone wrong, the *Cantos* were a masterpiece. *A mess,* Pound said. *Stupidity and ignorance all the way through.* But Pound's work had touched off the entire Modernist revolution in poetry. His grand plan to—Pound shook his head. His voice was rusty as an ancient child's. *The intention was bad,* he insisted. His eyes burned like blow torches. *That's the problem. Anything I've done has been an accident. Anything good has been spoiled by my intentions, my preoccupation with stupid and irrelevant things.*

Pound's anti-Semitism had been fucked up, Ginsberg agreed, but hadn't he paid? Like Prospero, he had broken his staff. He had drowned his book. Did he want to be the Messiah too? He'd have to be a Buddhist to be a perfect Messiah! The old man smiled, and Ginsberg placed his hand on Pound's talon. "But I'm a Buddhist Jew," Ginsberg said, "whose perceptions have been strengthened by the series of practical exact language models which are scattered throughout the *Cantos* like stepping stones—ground for me to occupy, to walk on—so despite your intentions, the practical effect has been to clarify my perceptions, even if all beauty is an accident. Now do you accept my blessing?" Pound hesitated, opening his mouth like an old turtle. *I do,* he said. *But my worst mistake was the stupid suburban prejudice of anti-Semitism. All along, that spoiled everything.* He squeezed Ginsberg's hand.

When Michael Reck published this conversation in the June 1968 issue of *Evergreen Review,* critics scoffed. What right did Ginsberg have to pardon Pound? Had the old man truly repented? Possibly not, but Ginsberg's blessing brought him some peace. During his solitary walks around Venice, he no longer dodged reporters or glared like a ruffled heron at photographers. Instead, he lost himself in the city's street life. Glassblowers shaped whimsical birds and fish for spectators and then smashed their entire menagerie without compunction. A *maddonaro,* a sidewalk artist, spent the entire day creating a chalk reproduction of Titian's Assumption, only to let pedestrians trample his drawing for a few coins. On the Lido, children repeatedly built sandcastles, squealing and clapping as the waves destroyed their work. Beauty doesn't need to be eternal. It doesn't need to save civilization. It doesn't even need a point. Keats said that he would gladly agonize all night over a poem, even if he knew that the first ray of dawn would set fire to the manuscript.

Who can lift the great ball of crystal? Pound had asked. *Who can enter the great acorn of light?* No one. Human beings are not demigods, not even geniuses. Once shattered, the rose window of civilization cannot be put together again. We cannot reassemble its fragments. We cannot even remove the slivers from our hide. This is a blessing. "The splinter in our eye," said Theodore Adorno, "is the best magnifying glass." We must see that the world has gone to pieces, and so have we. As the Psalmist says: "A broken and contrite heart, O God, you will not despise."

Ezra Pound died on All Saint's Day, 1972, at SS Giovanni e Paolo, Venice's municipal hospital. He was eighty-seven years old. The funeral at the Church of San Giorgio Maggiore was stark, fittingly so for a man who had described himself as "the last American living the tragedy of Europe." Pound had insisted that his casket be placed on the floor without cloth, candles, or incense. Four pallbearers carried it across Piazza San Marco in a dreary rain. A black gondola, decorated with six wreaths, took the body across the lagoon to the island cemetery of San Michele, where Pound was buried near Sergei Diaghilev and Igor Stravinsky.

☾

Today, Venice itself might be dying. As its population ebbs, its tides continue to rise. Waves have so badly eroded its infrastructure that the city is more fragile than antique glass. Will the world's most beautiful kaleidoscope shatter and sink into the sea?

To prevent this disaster, Consorzio Venezia (CVN), a consortium of powerful construction companies, is building seventy-eight underwater floodgates to shield the city from the Adriatic, but scandal swamped this project in June 2014 when Mayor Giorgio Orsoni, along with thirty-five public officials and contractors, were accused of skimming 20 million euros from public coffers.

Arrests and resignations followed. Brawls broke out in the town hall. For a year, Venice had no city government. Rome appointed a *commissario* to take over the office of mayor and dissolved the Magistrato alle Acque, the authority governing the lagoon. Adrift, Venetians wonder whether their city is doomed but still hunt for beauty in its alleys and canals.

"What else is there?" asks Diego Redolfi, who twenty years ago chucked his job as a hotel receptionist to join Venice's possibly last generation of gondoliers. Beauty, however, depends on skill as much as luck. "It's like making love," Redolfi says of his vanishing craft. "Sometimes you don't [master it] after a lifetime. But in the meantime, you can practice."

On Campo San Bartolomeo, beneath the statue of Carlo Goldoni, street musicians perform an old nursery rhyme. Or do they improvise nonsense to fool the tourists? Goldoni smiles. As a crowd swarms the shops and restaurants, the musicians sing this riddle:

Do you want to see what eyes have never seen?
Look at the moon.
Do you want to hear what ears have never heard?
Listen to the wind.
Do you want to touch what hands have never touched?
Pat the ground.

Acknowledgments

WE THANK THE EDITORS of the following anthology and journals for permitting us to include previously published work in this book:

ℰ *Others Will Enter at the Gates* (Black Lawrence Press, 2015),

ℰ *Feile-Festa, Ginosko, Hawai'i Review, Leaf Garden, OCHO, Pedestal, Scissors & Spackle, Sleepingfish, The Prose-Poem Project, Third Wednesday, Yellow Medicine Review,* and *Yemassee*

A version of the essay "The Eternal Children," originally titled "The Eternal Children Learn to Speak: Immigrants and Exiles as the Lost Boys of the New Millennium," was presented as a critical paper at "Exilic Capitals: The Cold War Exodus and Beyond," an academic seminar hosted by the American Comparative Literature Association (ACLA) at New York University (March 23, 2014).

About the Authors

Andrei Guruianu, born in 1979 in Bucharest, Romania, teaches in the Expository Writing Program at New York University. He is the author of more than a dozen books of poetry and prose, most recently *Made in the Image of Stones* and *Portrait Without a Mouth* (both from BrickHouse Books, 2014). Former U.S. Poet Laureate Ted Kooser has featured him in the column *American Life in Poetry*. Learn more about his life and work at www.andreiguruianu.com.

Anthony Di Renzo, a fugitive from advertising, teaches writing at Ithaca College. His books, such as *Bitter Greens: Essays on Food, Politics, and History from the Imperial Kitchen* (State University of New York Press, 2010) and *Trinàcria: A Tale of Bourbon Sicily* (Guernica Editions, 2013), satirize the ongoing culture war between Italian humanism and American business and technology. Italy usually loses. As Pasquino, Rome's talking statue, he contributes a column to San Francisco's *L'Italo-Americano*. He lives in Ithaca, New York, an Old World man in a New Age town.